FEAR
LESS

ALSO BY GAVIN DE BECKER

The Gift of Fear
Protecting the Gift

FEAR LESS

*Real Truth About
Risk, Safety, and
Security in a Time
of Terrorism*

■

GAVIN DE BECKER

Little, Brown and Company

BOSTON   NEW YORK   LONDON

First Edition

For information on AOL Time Warner Book Group's online
publishing program, visit www.ipublish.com.

ISBN 0-316-08596-0
LCCN 2001097790

10   9   8   7   6   5   4   3   2   1

Q–MART

Designed by Stratford Publishing Services

Printed in the United States of America

*This book is dedicated to the source
of courage within each of us — no matter how
each reader defines that source.*

CONTENTS

FEAR
LESS

THE ILLUSION OF POWERLESSNESS

S OON, ALL THE PLANNING would pay off and this odd double life would come to an end. A few people in the Florida cell had actually enjoyed living as Americans, but during refresher training in Europe, they were reminded that the United States was against everything they believed in.

The most committed among them found Americans objectionable, but it would be worth all the waiting and all the hating when news reached home that they had accomplished what was always believed to be impossible: striking America hard from within. Theirs was an enormous undertaking, far bigger than the sleeping giant would ever have dreamed, but the mission statement was simple: Start with several shocking blows at once, and then deliver grief in new ways for a long while.

Every day, their training proved its value: Know how to blend in, conceal your identity, learn the culture, read American newspapers, study the transportation system. Stay focused, and what you do will change everything.

It did change everything, though the top people in the operation would not live to see it happen.

These facts have become famous since September 11, 2001, but the story you just read is about another terrorist operation, one you likely never heard of, one that was discovered and completely neutralized by the FBI.

At first, federal officials were hesitant to believe the sheer ambition of the plot, but as they learned more they undertook one of America's largest manhunts — in total secrecy. At times during the case, members of several linked cells were spread all around the country, and FBI agents were fighting the calendar to stop the violence that was scheduled to begin on the Fourth of July. Only three weeks before that date, the full extent of the terror plan was uncovered, though it almost wasn't.

A young woman named Farrar Teeple was taking an evening walk along the wide, empty beach near her father's home on New York's Long Island. Some motion in the dunes caught her eye, and although the light was low, she could make out a group of men. Were they burying something in the sand? She strained to see. The cool night air turned abruptly cold for Farrar when the men suddenly stopped what they were doing, stood up straight, and stared toward her. They did not speak or move and neither did she. For a moment she tested the welcome thought that they didn't see her, but she had to let it go when one of the men broke from the group without a word to the others and walked stiffly in her direction. He waved a few times, beckoning her toward him, but instead she backed up, then turned and ran quickly home. Panting as she entered the house, she told her father what she'd seen, thinking he would call the police. Instead, he reassured her that nobody doing anything suspicious would have waved at her and that it was nothing to bother the police about. Reluctantly, she accepted her father's judgment, but her intuition knew something was very wrong, and her intuition was very right.

Another person on the beach that night, John Cullen (an American hero you've never heard of), acted more decisively on his intuition. He smelled something unusual in the briny air, a strong smell that drew him down the beach toward those same men that Farrar had seen. He thought it might be something burning, but as he got closer he felt certain it was the smell of diesel fuel. That made him curious, and his curiosity led him to call officials at a nearby Coast Guard station. The next morning, FBI agents searching the beach found what those silent men had hurriedly buried in the sand: boxes containing explosives, guns, ammunition, timers, shortwave radios, fuses disguised as pen-and-pencil sets, and devices that carried sulfuric acid. It was clear the terrorists planned to come back for those things later, but as federal agents knelt on the beach anxiously taking notes, the ruthless conspirators were already on a train bound for New York City. That's where they intended to carry out the instructions they'd been given: Detonate bombs in Jewish-owned department stores, place bombs on bridges from Queens to the Bronx, and cause terror and panic in any way you can.

FBI investigators unraveled the plan completely, and even solved the mystery of that smell of diesel. It was caused by something nearly unimaginable given that it was 1942: the submarine that had traveled from Nazi Germany to deposit those men on the beach. (Another Nazi sub had dropped a second team of terrorists at Ponte Verde Beach, Florida.) Within weeks, the FBI had conducted a series of secret raids, eventually arresting 192 people in several cities. They had prevented state-sponsored terrorism at its most frightening, given the state that did the sponsoring.

Some might assume that the foiled Nazi terrorist plan in the 1940s differs in fundamental ways from current terrorist operations, or that the world was a more innocent place then. Neither assumption is accurate.

I'll share the diabolical details of this thwarted terrorist operation — and others — in later chapters, but for now it can remind us that violent plots against America are not new and that even suicidal ones are not fated to succeed in every case.

After the terrible events of September 11, many people mistook our enemies for superhuman, when they were merely antihuman. Occasionally effective, to be sure, but our enemies are not powerful or ubiquitous. Those words more accurately describe us; we just forgot that for a while. It is sobering to acknowledge that we cannot protect all possible targets, but it is also true that our enemies cannot attack all possible targets. Conspiratorial behavior, scurrying in darkness, hiding behind false identification, pretending, relying upon surprise — these are the only strategies of battle for people who never, ever do actual battle. In that sense, it flatters them to call this a war. In another sense, though, it is a war, a war to be won through deploying more cleverness and intuition than our enemies.

Take, for example, the instructors at the Pan Am International Flight Academy in Eagan, Minnesota. They had a Middle Eastern student who said he wanted to learn to fly a jet but didn't want to learn about landing or taking off — skills most aspiring pilots are highly motivated to master. Because a couple of people listened to their intuition and called the FBI in August of 2001 (a month before our imaginations were so painfully expanded), and because the FBI took Zacarias Moussaoui into custody, we didn't have to find out the hard way exactly what it was he had in mind. It's fair to assume now that he was just a few weeks away from doing something terrible.

That's a frightening thought, but just one of many frightening thoughts you've had to host, so of course you've felt fear about terrorism. How could you not? Nobody could witness what you witnessed, even if through the small window of television, and not react with shock and fear. As I've reminded many victims of violence many times, your defense system is designed to send the fear signal when it perceives enormous danger — and your defense system had never before assessed anything quite like what happened on September 11, or what's been happening since.

Should you feel fear? The question is irrelevant, for there is no *should* about fear. Of course you will feel fear when there is reason to, like it or not. Fear is as fast as the jets, as hard as the buildings, as thick as the smoke, as undeniable as the rubble, and far more powerful than the hate and anger that brought them all together and tore them all apart right in front of your eyes.

Fear is, and is supposed to be. Start there, accept it, and give yourself some of the same compassion you've so willingly extended to others since September 11.

Yes, you had it better than many, but yours was still a profound personal experience of violence, and it would not be compassionate to expect anyone, including you, to have put events instantly into perspective. You had nothing to compare it to, and you couldn't get far enough away to see it in context. Even context itself was changed. Life could not be woven together that Tuesday with the same thread you had used on Monday. That alone is frightening, and can be enlightening — but not until after we've fully felt the fear.

We gave lots of attention to what we saw on television, but something was going on inside each of us as well. The human brain, nature's most miraculous accomplishment, is never more effective than when its host may be at risk. Then, all internal resources are marshaled: experience, imagination, industriousness, intellect, creativity, memory. The brilliant soldiers of intuition are given strict orders to guard the exits; nobody goes off duty until you get the answers to questions posed by every cell in your body: What does this event mean to safety? Am I going to be all right? Are we all going to be all right?

Of course you imagined a thousand terrors; that's where terrorism really happens: in the imagination. You placed yourself in those planes and in those buildings and imagined everything you could. You walked yourself through previously inconceivable emergencies. If you didn't do it consciously, you did it in your dreams. And even if you don't recall the dreams, they are in your cells nonetheless. For a while, the sound of an airplane overhead transported you to undesired destinations in the memory, and even the image of an airplane in an advertisement or the sight of one against a distant sky awakened unwelcome ghosts.

Skulking among the frightening outcomes you could conjure was one you'd never even considered: the weaponizing of jetliners. What do you do with that? While those afraid of flying can choose to stay off planes, it isn't possible for people to avoid all places on the ground that might be targeted. Terror that rains down unpredictably from the sky touches as delicate a place in our minds as terror that rises from the deep; to the psyche, jets become giant man-eating sharks racing toward us with sinister determination. You could try ordering these intruders out of your mind, but all the exits were closed. Terror got in, but none got out.

It is also profoundly disturbing to have a rageful, committed enemy that you cannot see advancing. A nation warring upon us would seem a luxury by comparison because a nation has a fixed place on the planet Earth, terrain and geography we can know, resources we can evaluate. And a nation — unlike suicidal individuals — has something to lose. In our present situation, no decisive or traditional victory is possible. In this war, there will be no captured beachhead upon which we can lay our fears to rest. So we are challenged to find safety and peace of mind in other ways.

Yet, peace of mind seems difficult given what's been occupying the national dialogue: viruses, chemicals, cockpit doors, anthrax spores, decontamination teams, water supplies, FBI warnings, vaccinations, explosive devices, subways, fighter jets, gas masks, box cutters.

Just try to build a world that feels safe with these materials and it collapses under its own weight. When the thoughts you'd normally banish seem vital to your survival, you're reluctant to turn them off — and it's harder still when fear is sprayed at you like tear gas from every TV newsroom on every channel nearly every hour of every day. Next up, another terrible thing from someone else's imagination. Next up, another expert in some terrible science. Next up, another nightmare.

In order to get back to day-to-day life, you've had to place events and information into some vague framework. But so many questions linger just beneath consciousness, and so many answers you settled on tentatively call out for affirmation. Who is right — the reassuring public official on the news or the alarming public official in the segment that follows?

It's too hard to be on duty without a break. It's too hard to keep up with every new risk. It's too hard to be anxious all the time. It's too damn hard.

It's stressful to live like this, and it is natural for tension to seek resolution. Stretch a rubber band and it snaps back when you let go — but never all the way. Stress and tension change things. This isn't good or bad: it just is. Change always carries opportunities, and one we have today is the possibility of becoming less controlled by unwarranted fear than we used to be.

The television news business may not welcome that outcome — but I think you do. You don't want panic or terror or needless worry, but you do want truth — whatever that truth may be — so you can organize all that's happened and what you've learned, and get some rest.

· · ·

Just as your imagination has placed you in frightening situations, it is now time to place yourself in empowering situations, time to see that you have a role to play, and contrary to so many TV news stories, it isn't just victim-in-waiting. Someone else may decide if you will be a target — but you decide whether or not you will be a victim.

The solution to worry is action, and it is time to address our fear fully so that it will stop nagging us. Your fear deserves to be answered, and you have the right to be safe, and to feel safe.

I don't mean a fraudulent feeling of safety made possible by denial, or a feeling promised by a politician or paid for with precautions that try to trick your defense system while doing nothing about actual danger. I mean a true, informed feeling of safety that comes from understanding violence, risk, intuition, fear, and security. Being safe and feeling safe are the destinations of this book, and I am committed to helping you get there. Then you'll help others get there too, for in the words of Nelson Mandela, "As we are liberated from our own fear, our presence automatically liberates others."

Being liberated from fears is a lofty goal. To get there I won't tell you there's nothing to be concerned about, or tell you not to worry. I am not a therapist. I am someone who has worked deep in the stuff of violence and fear every day for nearly three decades. My consulting firm's seventy associates and I help answer some of the highest-stakes questions that individuals and nations face. We are called in after a madman shoots a group of federal employees arriving to work one morning, and we are called when a media figure opens a letter and finds threats, or blood, or powder, or things far more disturbing than any of those. We interview assassins in prisons, advise the family of a slain foreign president, and track down and arrest stalkers. We assess death threats from would-be terrorists, mass killers, stalkers, angry employees, and aspiring assassins. The clients we advise include presidents (of countries and corporations), governors, mayors, police departments, movie stars, athletes, and religious leaders. We developed a computer-assisted threat-assessment system called MOSAIC that is used to screen threats to justices of the U.S. Supreme Court, as well as MOSAIC systems used by state police agencies protecting the governors of eleven states. We designed a MOSAIC system that's part of the process used to assess threats to members of Congress, and we've advised on the security of federal facilities, from the White

House gates to the first building you see as you drive into CIA headquarters. We help clients evaluate risk, reduce hazard, prevent violence, and manage fear.

Because I have protected people against IRA bombs in London, Middle Eastern extremists in Israel, and terrorist actions in Africa, and because of my sustained look at violence, I am called an expert. Indeed, I have learned many lessons, but my basic premise in these pages is that you too can be an expert at understanding violent behavior and assessing risk. Like every creature on earth, you can know when you are in the presence of danger. You have the gift of a brilliant internal guardian that stands ready to warn you of hazards and guide you through risky situations — a system that works best when accurately informed.

That's where I come in. For more than a year before the terrorist acts of September 11, I'd been working on a book about fear and risk in our society. It was to be my third on these topics, and though much of that book is relevant to our current situation, it was not due for many months. With the fear and the reality reaching the level of national emergency, I canceled, postponed, and set aside all I could to complete this book as quickly as possible. I am writing as a consultant, as if you walked into my office today with questions about violence, security, safety, precaution, prediction, risk, denial, and fear. Sometimes I'll have a lot to say; other times I might suggest you quit thinking so much. Above all, I commit to tell you the absolute truth as I see it, directly and fully, on topics about which people rarely tell the whole truth — and rarely want the whole truth.

For a long while, Americans had an illusion of complete safety from foreign enemies — and it's been shattered. We have replaced it with another illusion: that of complete vulnerability and powerlessness — and it too must be shattered.

Gas masks and canceled family trips, antidotes and survival gear, stockpiling food and staying at home — all choices I understand, but it's as if many Americans are preparing to be victims. America has bought into a false belief that there is little the average citizen can do about terrorism. Only government, many think, can detect and prevent terrorist acts, when in fact it is regular citizens who can do these things in ways that government on its own cannot.

Although a few Americans act as if they are preparing to be casualties of war, the truth is they are fully qualified to be part of the antiterrorism effort. You don't have to do hand-to-hand combat to defeat people whose success depends entirely upon not being found out. Before the courageous FBI raid, before the arrest, long before the news conference, there is a regular American citizen who sees something that seems suspicious, listens to intuition, and has the character to risk being wrong or seeming foolish when making the call to authorities.

Conspiratorial planning and preparation do not often occur in the view of FBI agents. They occur most often in the view of regular citizens, and for every law-enforcement officer on the front lines, there can be a hundred citizens providing observations and information —

if they understand enough about the planning and the pre-incident indicators of terrorism.

For example, at a flight school in Florida, two men from the Middle East paid a lot of money to use a commercial-jet simulator even though they had logged nowhere near enough training hours to actually fly commercial aircraft. It was not a joyride, for they were stern faced as they focused most of their time on steering. It might seem outrageous now that nobody called officials about Mohamed Atta and Marwan Al-Shehhi, but in fairness, the folks at the Florida flight school were among thousands of Americans who had literally thousands of encounters with the men who committed the mass murders of September 11.

What are terrorists likely to do next? Something surprising, and then something mundane, then something predictable, and then something surprising again. Whatever it is, you and other Americans will be able to handle it, and in many cases, you'll be able to stop it from happening.

Heroism today is learning about how terrorism works. That's part of your contribution to the nation and to yourself. To do this well, our courage will have to be placed ahead of our denial.

With denial, the details we need for the best predictions float silently by us like life preservers, and though the man overboard may enjoy the comfortable belief that he is still in his stateroom, there is soon a price to pay for his daydream. Americans now know the price, and it is too high.

Though I won't flinch from reality, this book is not a compendium of every risk you might face. You've gotten enough of that, and my work is far too practical to participate in melodrama. I won't try to talk you out of anything you feel or into anything someone might think you should feel. I want only what you want for yourself: enhanced safety and freedom from unwarranted fear.

While I'll look at both sides of some government decisions, I'll honor this truth: Our political leaders have been and will be faced with stunningly difficult choices. All Americans have strong feelings about security, civil liberties, war, and a thousand other ideological issues that divide us, but for my purposes here, there is no controversy. If I feel a popular security precaution is a waste of time, I'll tell you so. If something a government official says strikes me as just silly, I'll tell you so. If, in my view, there are things the airline industry could easily be doing to enhance safety, I'll tell you so. If I see people intentionally frightening you for their own profit, I'll tell you so.

I want merely to provide some tools you might not be aware of and to share my experience to help you answer these questions:

Can air travel be safe?
Can the government detect and prevent future
    terrorist acts?
Why didn't the FBI stop the 9/11 hijackers?
What can the nation do to reduce risk?
How can we best talk to our children about what
    has happened and what might happen?
What can individuals do to reduce fear and worry?

What can individuals do to reduce terrorism in
    America?
What are terrorists likely to do next?

Most simply, is everything going to be all right?

I can answer that last question right now: If you define
"all right" as meaning freedom from all violence and risk,
the answer is no, everything is not going to be all right,
because everything has never been all right.

The energy of violence has always moved through our
culture, and all others. Some experience it as a light but
unpleasant breeze, easy to tolerate. Others are destroyed
by it, as if by a hurricane. But nobody — nobody — is
untouched. Violence is a part of America, and more than
that, it is a part of our species. It is around us and it is in us.
As the most powerful people in history, we have climbed
to the top of the world food chain, so to speak, and until
recently, we'd come to believe that no predator or enemy
posed any danger of consequence. We are now ready to
look at that differently.

Start by recalling that violence is a force of nature, a
permanent and regular feature of mankind — and it is not
new. In this sense, our world is exactly as it always was.

For example, in 1984 members of a cult contaminated
salad bars at ten restaurants in Oregon. There were nearly
eight hundred casualties. Did you even know about this?

In 1986 a heavily armed couple with a bomb took 150
students and adults hostage at an elementary school in
Wyoming. They shot one teacher in the back as he tried

to flee. They demanded $300 million to release the students, but the plan fell apart when the bomb accidentally exploded, killing the woman. The man then shot himself to death in front of the children, seventy-four of whom were seriously injured by the blast of the gasoline bomb. Did you even hear about this horrendous incident?

In 1995 police investigators aborted a massive plot to blow up twelve jetliners as they crossed the Pacific, crash a plane into CIA headquarters, and assassinate the pope. Did you even hear about this diabolical plan before September 11? Would you have believed it possible?

On a recent Christmas Eve, powerful bombs went off in ten different cities. At the time, it was an unprecedented terrorist event, astonishing — but it did not astonish you. You didn't know it was going on because it happened in Indonesia.

So, is everything going to be all right? Of course not. Never was. Never is. Never will be.

Are you going to be all right? Yes, you are. I am as certain of that as one can be of anything that involves human beings.

I could say that no building you are in will be hit by a plane, no plane you are on will be hijacked, and no biological or chemical attack will affect you. Though the odds are overwhelmingly high that I am correct, your defense system is hardly willing to take my word for it so easily.

So let's look briefly at just one of the risks that concerns Americans: commercial air travel. I believe with substantial certainty that the hijacking of commercial jets the way it's been done in the past is just that: a thing of the past. *It is over.* For forty years, hijackers gained the cooperation and compliance of passengers through the promise of safety or the threat of harm. Neither of those promises will work anymore.

Regular citizens now constitute the lowest-tech and most effective element of security on airliners. All the meticulous searches, National Guardsmen, X-ray machines, questions at ticket counters, metal detectors, double checking of IDs, and confiscating of nail clippers don't equal the effectiveness of a few passengers willing to act decisively when someone tries to gain unauthorized access to the cockpit. The murderers of 9/11 likely did not know they had committed the hijackings to end all hijackings. But that's what happened as Americans viewed and re-viewed history's most effective training video — produced by the terrorists themselves.

There can be comfort in knowing that you are a capable part of an effective security system as opposed to a halfhearted participant in something that's always been a bit of a sham. You can invest confidence when relying upon yourself — just as you're at ease when you're in the driver's seat but a bit anxious when somebody else is at the wheel.

All governments on earth want you to believe that only they can protect you, but our government is us, and just as we need its help, it needs ours. In short, working together is now the only reasonable way. In chapter 7, I'll explore air security in much more detail, providing some information that may astound you. But for now, I want only to make the point that when accurately informed and not deprived of the opportunity for responsibility, each American can participate in national security with brilliant effectiveness. That happened on United Airlines Flight 93 when the passengers decisively took the plane away from men who would use it for mass murder. By sad circumstance, the Americans on Flight 93 got their accurate information late, but you'll have yours in plenty of time.

We have been through many enormous tragedies, and in the next chapter, I'll offer some perspective by discussing what we've survived and how we did it. In chapter 3, I'll share some of what I've learned about the inner workings of fear and its role in our natural defense system. I'll show how to tell the difference between true fear, a survival signal we want because it sounds an alarm in the presence of danger, and unwarranted fear, a destructive impostor. In chapters 4 and 5, I'll explore the architecture of criminal conspiracy and provide specific ways that you and other Americans can see pre-incident indicators early enough to make a difference.

Chapter 6 will load your intuition with practical information about biological and chemical terrorism, risk assessment, and threat assessment. Chapter 7 will focus on the key parts of airline security.

The nature of terrorism is that it creates uncertainty by changing its expression. Whatever happens, however, you and other Americans will be better able to handle it by taking all you learn and crafting a world that feels safe for yourself and your family. That goal is complicated by fear's primary delivery system: television news. Often it's hard to find the not-so-alarming information that's obscured by the oh-so-alarming presentation. Chief among the skills we now need to stay focused on what matters is the ability to tell the difference between a newsroom act and an important fact. In chapters 8 and 9, I'll present ways to be better armored against news tactics and to help keep your mind clear so you can feel safer and be safer.

Sometimes a violent act is so frightening that we call the perpetrator a monster, but as you'll see in chapter 10, it is by finding our shared humanness — his similarity to you and me — that we can gain the most useful insight. On this there is much to learn, including how to live with what we learn.

So, here's the map for this journey: We'll start by putting our present situation into the context of things we've experienced in the past. Then I'll discuss how fear works — at its best and at its worst. With that foundation, we'll look at what you can do about terrorism and then study some of the specific hazards we're facing today. I'll share ideas about how to get information without being scared half to death in the process, and finally we'll look at some truths about human beings who act violently. If you stay with me — through both the hard truths and the reassuring ones — I feel certain you'll be better prepared for the times ahead of us.

You and I can be sources of reasoned information, insight, comfort, and courage. The more of us there are, the better. And though we may not be able to stop all terror-*ism,* we can stop a lot of the terror. So let's go further into the relevant topics than one can do in a sound bite, go into them without alarming bulletins and scary graphics, go into them without hype or politics, go into them just deeply enough to come out the other side.

Then you can see if you reach the same conclusions I have: that you can find your life in these times, that you can influence your own safety, that you can help protect your country, that you can manage fear, and that you are going to be all right.

CHANGED FOREVER,
FOREVER THE SAME

*Vitality shows not only in the ability to persist,
but in the ability to start over.*

— F. SCOTT FITZGERALD

THE EVENTS OF 9/11 were of mythic scale: so many lives lost, so many more lost for a time to grief, the utter destruction, the starkness of fierce hatred, the vulnerability of the government — even the supposedly all-protecting military wasn't safe. Much that we had chosen to believe was proven false all on the same day: that airports are secure, great buildings are strong and permanent, an airline captain is always in charge of his plane, a pilot's skill is special, the perpetrators of attention-capturing acts want to survive and experience their notoriety.

Since that day we've had to let go of plenty of old beliefs, so that in addition to everything else, we have experienced the death of denial.

Denial is the psychological defense mechanism we unconsciously deploy to make unpleasant truths go away, but on September 11 those defenses were breached, leaving millions of people overwhelmed by terrifying ideas and feelings. It was, right from the start, difficult to persuade yourself that each incident was isolated, or that the danger would pass. The usual search for answers was stalled; the trauma was so profound that your mind would not accept a simple solution. The story couldn't be wrapped up merely by the identifying of a villain, even a media-age supervillain like Osama bin Laden. Firing missiles could not right the sheer upside-down-ness of what happened, and was continuing to happen.

My goal in this chapter is to show that even when we thought things were right side up, there were plenty of dangers we had successfully compartmentalized. We are challenged to do that again now. To compartmentalize is not to deny; it is to acknowledge the reality of something, look right at it, and place it, literally, in a mental compartment, in a kind of quarantine, separated from our moment-to-moment thinking in such a way that we can manage life. The theory here is to change what we can change and accept what we cannot change. Violence is one of those things we cannot change; it is always present. What differs is the expression of violence, but violence itself has remained a constant throughout human history.

That may be a saddening or discouraging thought at first, but in the truth lies relief for those who anxiously wonder about whether there will be more violence. There is nothing to wonder about. We live in a nation with its own violence epidemic, remember? In the past two years alone, more Americans died from gunshot wounds than were killed during the entire Vietnam War — ten times the number who died at the World Trade Center. Many people in other countries believe ours to be the most frightening place to live, and some startling contrasts support their view.

For example, in all of Japan, the number of young men shot to death in a year is equal to the number killed in New York City in a single busy weekend. By this time tomorrow, four hundred Americans will suffer a shooting injury, and more than a thousand will face a criminal with a gun. When four jumbo jets crashed on September 11 we were deeply shaken, but imagine that a jumbo jet full of passengers crashed every single month, month in and month out. The number of people killed still wouldn't equal the number of American women murdered by their husbands and boyfriends each year. None of that is comforting, I know, but it does provide some frame of reference.

Just as violence has been a constant, so has fear. It's as if we keep a space in our collective mind reserved for things that frighten us, and that space must be kept occupied. If we are not fearing terrorism, it's mad cow disease, or killer bees, or gas-tank fires, or dangerous tires. Before September 11, we feared enemies within: AIDS, asbestos, the vengeful co-worker, the local serial killer, the home invasion robber, the rampaging high school student.

A *USA Today* poll about what Americans feared revealed a catalog of catastrophes right off the TV news: 20 percent of Americans reported a fear of being in an air crash; 18 percent were afraid of being a victim of mass violence. These fears collided on September 11, and though

I know the percentages would be higher today, my point is that these fears are not new.

After worrying for so long about dreaded outcomes that never come, when a truly terrible thing happens, it can confirm our worst fears. Each frightening disaster rekindles the sense of insecurity and joins all the other frightening things in our memory. Because it gets attached to other traumas, the latest risk is always perceived as the greatest risk.

But is it the greatest risk?

It may be that most of us are in no more danger today than we were on September 10, 2001 — but we are focusing on different dangers now. We had found ways to live with the old familiar risks, often by denying them. Americans are, after all, experts at denial, a choir whose song could be titled "Things Like That Don't Happen in This Neighborhood."

Certainly denial can be seductive, but it has an insidious side effect. For all the peace of mind deniers think they get by saying it isn't so, the fall they take when faced with new violence is all the more unsettling. Denial is a save-now-pay-later scheme, a contract written entirely in small print, for in the long run the denying person knows the truth on some level, and it causes a constant low-grade anxiety. Millions of people who repressed that anxiety have now had the thin protective bubble popped, and they are among those who feel most vulnerable today. I do not propose a continuation of denial — for it never serves safety — but I do propose compartmentalization of those risks that appear frequently in our imaginations and only occasionally in our reality. See the risks, address those we can, and quarantine the rest.

Understand that one person's old familiar risk can be another person's absolute terror. Londoners visiting Los Angeles ask in disbelief about carjacking: "You mean he looks you in the eye, aims a handgun at your face, and says he'll kill you if you don't get out of the car?" And we say how rare it is, how most times they just take the car and that's it, how it happened to a friend and she's fine, and anyway, we add offhandedly, we're insured. Then we visit London and ask, "You mean you go out for a night on the town knowing full well that an IRA bomb could go off at any moment?" And they tell us that recent bombs haven't been very powerful anyway, and even with the really big ones, the main risk is the broken glass flying around and not the blast itself.

Do you know what Israelis do after a bomb explodes on a passenger bus bound for Tel Aviv? The next morning, people line up to get on the bus to Tel Aviv. That's a statement of courage they choose to make, a refusal to be terrorized — and yet there are risks you take for granted that would make those same people hesitate. For example, the rate of firearm deaths in the United States is five times higher than it is in Israel.

Given all that's happened, however, most Americans do feel less safe than they did growing up. But let's look at that safer world of our youth:

For most of us, it was a world without air bags or mandatory seat belts, before the decrease in smoking, before early detection of cancer, before CAT scan, ultrasound, organ transplant, amniocentesis, and coronary bypass surgery, before 911 systems showed police and paramedics your address. You remember those oh-so-safe sixties, when angry world powers planned nuclear attack, and schoolchildren practiced regular air-raid drills. Sure, balled up under the desk at six years old, listening intently for the whistle of an incoming missile sent by a powerful enemy who hated us — ah, those were the safe days.

Still, many Americans understandably compare their fears of today to an idealized past, longing to get back the lives — and the risks — they were used to. For them, it might be helpful to recall that we didn't feel all that safe before 9/11.

We were searched for weapons before boarding a plane, visiting city hall, going to court, seeing a television show taping, attending a speech by the President, and even entering some high schools. Government buildings were already surrounded by barricades, and we wrestled through so-called tamperproof packaging to get a couple of aspirin. All of this was triggered by the deeds of fewer than ten dangerous men who got our attention by frightening us. What other quorum in American history, save those who wrote our Constitution, could claim as much impact on our day-to-day lives? Now, as we add Mohamed Atta to the list, let's recall that we have already prevailed in the face of other huge, paradigm-shifting events:

- Puerto Rican terrorists burst into Congress and shot five elected officials in 1954.

- The President was shot and killed in 1963, and within minutes, just about every person on the planet Earth knew about it. It was the media age's first example of how a trauma can be simultaneously shared by billions of people.

- In 1962 the United States detected nuclear missiles in Cuba and went toe-to-toe with the Soviet Union, and all the fears of the atomic age became real. Millions of families stockpiled food, dug makeshift bomb shelters in their backyards, and waited for nuclear war.

- In 1968 two loved leaders were assassinated, presidential front-runner Robert Kennedy and civil rights legend Martin Luther King, Jr. King's murder sparked riots that led millions of Americans to doubt whether the violence could be contained by police.

- In 1969 followers of Charles Manson committed two separate multiple murders in upscale Los Angeles neighborhoods, torturing and killing several well-known people on the same night. The brutal murder spree exposed an anti-establishment cult that conjured fear in the public and changed America from a place where people left their homes unlocked to the place it is today.

- In 1978 followers of cult leader Jim Jones shot and killed U.S. congressman Leo Ryan and four congressional staff members. Jim Jones then presided over a mass suicide in which more than *nine hundred* people died together by consuming cyanide.

- In 1979 an accident occurred at the Three Mile Island nuclear power plant, resulting in an evacuation of all people within a five-mile radius. The plant remains closed to this day.
- Someone put lethal poison in bottles of Tylenol, leading to seven deaths and causing Americans to doubt that the products in their homes were safe. This single event has changed virtually every bottle and jar we touch.
- In 1986 the space shuttle *Challenger* blew up before our eyes, leading to a period of shared mourning and sadness, and a loss of faith in our long-established technological leadership.
- In the early eighties, a lethal new communicable disease arrived in our social consciousness: AIDS. Aside from killing 30 million people, it changed dating habits and sexual behavior and led to some acceptance and lots of rejection of alternative lifestyles.
- Two hundred forty-one marines were killed when a terrorist drove a massive truck bomb into the U.S. Marine headquarters in Beirut.
- In 1986 the world experienced its worst nuclear accident, at Chernobyl: 135,000 people were evacuated from a twenty-square-mile area (hundreds of villages remain abandoned or buried to this day), helicopters dumped five thousand tons

of clay to smother the burning reactor — and still thousands of people died and hundreds of thousands experienced health consequences.

- A terrorist bomb blew up an American jetliner over Lockerbie, Scotland. All 259 people on board were killed, as were eleven on the ground.
- The World Trade Center was bombed by Middle Eastern terrorists who left a massive truck bomb in the underground parking lot. Six people were killed, more than a thousand injured.
- One hundred sixty-seven people were killed and more than five hundred injured when the federal building in Oklahoma City was destroyed by a terrorist's bomb (a homegrown terrorist incident — the type for which we seem to have greater tolerance).
- A fifteen-year-old Oregon boy murdered his parents, then went to school and shot twenty-four people.
- Two boys, one just eleven years old, pulled the fire alarm at their Jonesboro, Arkansas, school and shot fourteen people as they exited the building.
- Two students placed thirty bombs in and around Columbine High School, then shot thirty-five students and one teacher. Each boy then committed suicide. This story dominated the attention of the nation for months, even though there have been more than one hundred incidents of multiple-victim shootings at schools since 1970.

How did we get through all these frightening things that happened to us? In cases where the incidents appeared unconnected to anything, the fear was brief. For example, after the nine-hundred-person suicide by followers of cult leader Jim Jones, we concluded accurately that it was an isolated incident — incomprehensible and bizarre, but of no continuing relevance to our safety. In the case of Chernobyl, the awesome event was little felt in America because the Soviet Union's iron curtain limited the flow of news. With AIDS, by far the biggest killer on the list, we changed what is within our grasp to change (our own behaviors), we educated people, and we undertook to improve understanding and treatment of the disease. Whether or not we do enough research, public education, or patient care is open to discussion, but it's clear we have acknowledged the presence of AIDS in our lives.

The way we took in the explosion of the space shuttle *Challenger* is similar in several ways to our experience of the events of 9/11. We all saw both of these shocking things happen — many of us at the instant they occurred. Just as buildings are expected always to stand, the space shuttle was expected always to fly — and the *Challenger* mission was perceived as even more safe than others because it carried grammar-school teacher Christa McAuliffe, a civilian selected by NASA to travel into space. We had seen so many launches before, so many spacecraft lifted on giant clouds of white smoke, that when something appeared to go differently with the *Challenger,* when the smoke changed, when the plume of fire seemed a bit too intense, we assumed we must be interpreting it incorrectly.

But, as with 9/11, millions of people had a horrible realization at the exact same instant: that we really had seen what we had just seen, and that it really did mean what it seemed to mean.

You can ask anyone about their feelings when the *Challenger* exploded, and what they describe will resonate with you. That's also true for the events of 9/11.

Even though we all saw the shuttle disaster, it didn't spark the same fear as the events of 9/11 for several reasons: First, our measure of acceptable risk is different for space travel; it's dangerous — we know it and the astronauts knew it. Second, the tragedy was seen as an aberration and a contained event, whereas the events of 9/11 were seen as the start of something new and terrible. And third, only a few died on the space shuttle, while thousands died at the World Trade Center. Tragedies that kill many people together stimulate an atavistic fear that the whole village will be wiped out. The village sends one man on a risky trip across the desert to search for water; they don't all go. An aging woman or man dies, okay; a hunter is killed by a large animal, okay — the village goes on. But when something threatens to wipe us all out, the internal guards that protect the integrity of genetic lines go on high alert.

There are other types of occurrences to which we respond without fear, and those usually involve risks we have already been able to compartmentalize. For example, a terrorist act overseas in which Americans are killed gets filed in the mind according to the seemingly harsh logic of personal survival: Terrorist Act, Middle Eastern Perpetrators,

Victims Knew the Risks, Happens Often, Not to Me, Easy to Avoid.

Today, instead of making our fears universal (seeing danger everywhere), we have the opportunity to place risks into manageable boxes, just as we have done before. When you put something in a box, you can keep your eye on it and stay connected to it, but you can't do that with things that overwhelm your whole world.

To maintain a sense of safety, we each have the ability to create in our mind a distance — a protective zone between ourselves and whatever horrifying incident threatens us. We haven't done that yet with terrorism because it is so hard to compartmentalize that which changes. It will be easier if we think of violence as violence, and not perceive each new costume it wears as if concealing something entirely new. As I'll explore in coming chapters, the same violence is always underneath.

For example, American-bred terrorists do terrible things from time to time, yet they don't scare us as much as terrorists from the Middle East do. This is because we feel that even if we catch and stop one Muslim extremist, somebody will replace him. And that is so. With a Boston Strangler, Son of Sam killer, or Night Stalker, we think it will end when we catch the one person. *And that is not so.* Somebody will replace him, too. Somebody will come next: a Hillside Strangler, Unabomber, Timothy McVeigh. I suggest you not think of perpetrators of violence as people we are imminently about to eradicate, almost done with, just one more criminal to catch. There is no inoculation against violence. People will continue to plan acts of extraordinary violence, and to really work toward prevention we must accept that these people are included in the "we" of humanity and are not interlopers who somehow sneaked in.

Before 9/11, many felt that they didn't need to learn too much about violence because the police would handle it, the government would handle it. But now, with the death of denial, we know that violence touches us all and belongs to us all. We have some learning to do, some preparation of new compartments into which we can place our anxieties.

In the meantime, during the adjustment period, to be prepared for something, you must predict it, at least in the general sense. To predict something, you must believe it is at least possible. The more likely we believe an outcome is, the better prepared we tend to make ourselves. So, even if it's sad to think of violence as a constant, acceptance of reality is always the highest ground you can find — and the safest — because from there you can see what's coming. From there, you can evaluate risks and organize defenses. From there, you can hear the messengers of intuition, the powerful and effective force at the center of your natural survival system.

· 3 ·

YOUR NATURAL
SURVIVAL SYSTEM

Technology is not going to save us. Our computers,
our tools, our machines are not enough. We have to
rely on our intuition, our true being.

— JOSEPH CAMPBELL

IN TIMES LIKE THESE, some may feel vulnerable and
without defenses, but nature's investment in each of
us is far too great for such an oversight. You have an astonishing defense system, brilliant beyond imagination —
because it operates, in fact, beyond imagination.

The brain built for protecting us was field-tested for
millions of years in the wild. I call it the wild brain, in
contrast with the logic brain so many people revere. The
logic brain is plodding and unoriginal. It is burdened with
judgment, slow to accept reality, and spends valuable energy
thinking about how things ought to be, used to be, or
could be. The logic brain has strict boundaries and laws
it wants to obey, but the wild brain obeys nothing, con-
forms to nothing, answers to nobody, and will do whatever it takes.

The wild brain is unfettered by emotion or politics, and as illogical as the wild brain may sometimes seem, it is, in the natural order of things, completely logical. It just doesn't care to convince us of anything by using logic. In fact, it doesn't give a damn what we think. Freed from the bonds of judgment, married only to perception, it carries us to observations and insight we later marvel at. Driving it all is intuition, the force that links us to the natural world and to our nature.

The root of the word *intuition, tuere,* means "to guard, to protect," and that is what it can do for us — more effectively than government, in fact more effectively than any other force on earth.

In coming chapters, I'll discuss some very specific aspects of terrorist planning that regular citizens might encounter, and which, if recognized, can be acted upon. Much of this recognition will happen intuitively as opposed to logically.

The intuitive system works best when free of the distractions of worry and anxiety — and that blessed outcome is more likely to occur if you fully understand how fear works. These issues are explored in greater detail in my book *The Gift of Fear,* but for now, let's look at a few of the concepts that can help reduce anxiety about danger.

It may be hard to accept the importance of intuition, because it is usually looked upon by us thoughtful Western beings with contempt. It is often described as emotional, unreasonable, or inexplicable. Some husbands chide their wives about "feminine intuition" and don't take it seriously.

If intuition is used by a woman to explain some choice she made or a concern she can't let go of, those men roll their eyes and write it off. They much prefer logic — the grounded, explainable, unemotional thought process that ends in a supportable conclusion. In fact, most Americans worship logic, even when it's wrong, and deny intuition, even when it's right.

At just the moment when our intuition is most basic, people tend to consider it amazing or supernatural. A woman tells a simple story as if it were mystical: "I absolutely knew when the phone rang that it would be my college roommate, calling after all these years." Though people act as if predictions of who is calling are miraculous, they rarely are. In this case, her old roommate was reminded of her by reports of the explosion of the space shuttle. Is it a miracle that both women happened to watch the same news event along with a billion others? Is it a miracle that their strongest association with space travel was the angry belief they shared in college that women would never be astronauts? And a woman astronaut died in the space shuttle explosion that morning, and the two women thought of each other, even after a decade.

Men, of course, have their own version of intuition. Theirs is more viscerally named a "gut feeling," but it isn't just a feeling. For both men and women, intuition sparks a process more extraordinary in the natural order than the most fantastic computer calculation. It is our most complex cognitive process and, at the same time, the simplest. It is the knowing without knowing why; it is making the journey from *A* to *Z* without stopping at any other letter along the way.

Because society has trained us to believe that we can't protect ourselves, that we don't know the answers, that officials and professionals know what's best, we have come to believe that we will find certainty outside ourselves. We won't, of course, but we can find the illusion of certainty, particularly if that's what we're willing to settle for. When the airline employee dismisses our concerns about the odd behavior of three passengers waiting to board a flight, our hesitation may be the only thing that stands between us and a false feeling of certainty. That hesitation stands there for a reason, and we won't always find the reason with logic.

Whenever we perceive anything unusual, there's a question our natural defense system always asks automatically: Is there danger here? In *A Natural History of the Senses,* author Diane Ackerman says, "When we see an object, the whole peninsula of our senses wakes up to appraise the new sight. All the brain's shopkeepers consider it from their point of view, all the civil servants, all the accountants, all the students, all the farmers, all the mechanics." We could add the soldiers and guards to Ackerman's list, for it is they who evaluate the context in which things occur, the appropriateness and significance of literally everything we perceive. They discard the irrelevant (when they can identify it) and value the meaningful. They recognize the survival signals we don't even (consciously) know are signals.

Intuition has many messengers (several of which will be explored in chapter 3), but the clearest and most urgent is fear. Nothing in life gets attention as reliably as fear — and that's the way the system is designed to work. Fear does some miraculous things when we perceive that we are in the presence of danger. First, it gets our bodies ready for action with a dose of adrenaline. It heats up the lactic acid in our muscles for running or fighting, and it even gives us a chemical called cortisol that makes our blood clot more quickly in case we're cut in a fight.

It's an amazing system designed to be a brief signal that gets you to listen, address the risk, and move on. The problem is that these chemicals are toxic, and in America, even more so since the tragic events of 9/11, lots of people are living in fear.

Our imaginations can be the fertile soil in which worry and anxiety grow from seeds to weeds, but when we assume an imagined outcome is a sure thing, we are in conflict with what Proust called an inexorable law: "Only that which is absent can be imagined." In other words, what you imagine cannot be happening in your presence right now, for if it were, you would perceive it. Similarly, the very fact that you fear something is solid evidence that it is not happening in your presence right now.

Fear summons powerful predictive resources that tell us what might come next. It is that which might come next that we fear — what might happen, not what is happening now. A literal example helps demonstrate this: As you stand near the edge of a high cliff, you might fear getting too close. If you stand right at the edge, you no longer fear getting too close, you now fear falling. To carry this all the way, if you fall, you no longer fear falling — you now fear landing. When compared with landing, falling isn't so bad.

This reminds me of a friend who used to be afraid of flying because of turbulence. After the four simultaneous hijackings, he told me, "Turbulence now makes me grateful. It reminds me that there are much worse things."

People use the word *fear* to describe so many feelings that are not fear, so I'll define our terms:

FEAR

- True fear is a signal in the presence of danger. It is always based upon something we perceive, something in our environment or our circumstance.
- Unwarranted fear is always based upon our memory or our imagination.

Imagine, for example, that you are about to board a flight when you are suddenly overtaken with dread and uncertainty about the pilot's ability to fly the plane. If the dread is based on a news story you saw three weeks ago about airlines hiring inexperienced pilots, it is unwarranted fear. If the fear is based upon seeing the pilot stumble out of the airport bar, it's the real thing. True fear is the messenger that intuition sends when the situation is urgent, and it's not easily quieted. If you want it to leave you alone, whatever questions it poses must be answered fully and credibly.

The challenge in dealing with the anxiety caused by terrorist acts is that answers are hard to come by. Uncertainty is a key component of terrorism; we are left to wonder what might happen next, to what degree, and where. The lack of predictability predictably causes anxiety, which, unlike true fear, is always caused by uncertainty.

ANXIETY

Anxiety is caused, ultimately, by predictions in which you have little confidence. Imagine that you are anxious because of signs that you might be fired: Co-workers act oddly toward you, and your boss is reluctant to commit you to any assignment. But these signs could also mean you are getting a promotion. When you are certain a prediction is correct, certain, for example, that you are about to be fired, you don't have anxiety about being fired. You might have anxiety about the things you can't predict with certainty, such as the ramifications of losing the job.

Predictions in which you have high confidence free you to respond, prepare, adjust, accept, feel sadness, or do whatever is needed. Accordingly, anxiety is reduced by improving the quality of your predictions. Higher quality predictions increase certainty, and *certainty is the antidote to anxiety*. It's worth doing, because the word *anxiety*, like the word *worry*, stems from a root that means "to choke," and that is just what it does to us.

WORRY

Worry is the fear we manufacture — it is not authentic, and it is not part of our defense system. If you look out the window and see lava from the local volcano slowly making its way toward your house, you don't worry, you run.

Unlike true fear, worry is a choice. Most often, people worry because it provides some secondary reward. There are many variations, but here are a few of the most popular reasons people worry:

- Worry is a way to avoid change; when we worry, we don't do anything about the matter.
- Excessive worry helps some people deal with matters they cannot influence. Powerlessness is one of the hardest things to admit, and there comes a point with risk where we have to do just that. Worry helps fight off that dreadful feeling that there's nothing we can do, because worrying feels like we are doing something.
- You've likely known someone who worried so much that people stopped telling that person anything. "Don't worry your mother" or "I'm worried half to death" are phrases that serve worriers by offering protection from too much reality.
- Worry can be a cloying way to have connection with others, the idea being that to worry about someone shows love. As many worried-about people will tell you, worry is a poor substitute for love or for taking loving action.

- Worry is a way to rehearse dreaded outcomes so that if they occur, the worrier believes he will be more prepared. Of course, it doesn't work. Worry simply gives people some of the very same consequences they'd get if the dreaded outcome occurred — while doing nothing constructive to prevent anything bad from happening. Worrying is not the same as planning; it is not an effective security precaution.

Worry is a choice, but true fear is involuntary; it will come and get your attention if necessary. But if a person feels fear constantly, there is no signal left for when it's really needed. Thus, the person who chooses to worry all the time or to persistently chew on unwarranted fears is actually making himself less safe. Worry is not a precaution; it is the opposite because it delays and discourages constructive action, and *action is the antidote to worry*.

In *Emotional Intelligence,* Daniel Goleman concludes that worrying is a sort of "magical amulet" that some people feel wards off danger. They believe that worrying about something will stop it from happening. He also correctly notes that most of what people worry about has a low probability of occurring, because we tend to take action about those things we feel are likely to occur. This means that very often the mere fact that you are worrying about something is a predictor that it isn't likely to happen.

When you worry yourself into an artificial fear about terrorism, you distract yourself from what is actually happening in favor of what you imagine might happen. Since the human imagination is powerful, you can conjure quite a litany of possibilities. Anytime you ask yourself the question "Could this happen?" the answer will be yes — because anything *could* happen, but there are better questions, such as "Will this happen?" or "*Is* this happening?"

Is worry an intuitive signal? In a roundabout way, it can be. That's because what we choose to worry about, however bad, is usually easier to look at than some other, less palatable issue. For this reason, a good exercise when worrying is to ask yourself, "What am I choosing not to see right now?" Worry may well be distracting you from something important. For example, someone might worry about unseen terrorists (What will they do next? Do operatives live nearby? Are they engaged in something dastardly right now?), while at the same time choosing not to register that she's seen someone videotaping the nuclear power plant several days in a row.

Worry, wariness, anxiety, and concern all have a purpose, but they are not fear. So any time a feeling isn't a signal in the presence of danger, then it really shouldn't be confused with fear. It may well be something worth trying to understand and manage, but it is not likely to be directly relevant to your present safety.

Worry will not help you answer the fundamental question that is on everyone's mind right now:

IS IT SAFE?

Since September 11, many people have asked me many questions: "Are terrorists more likely to strike in the day or at night?" "My husband works at a power plant; is he safe at work?" "There is a Muslim mosque near my son's school; should we transfer him somewhere else?" "Is it safe to visit a theme park?" "Is it safe to fly?" "We had tickets to the ball game; do you think the stadium is a terrorist target?" "I was planning to go to Boston for a family get-together, but we heard about a threat to Boston; should I cancel?"

Some might say questions like these cannot be answered, but every one can be answered and will be answered — though not always with great certainty.

In order to determine whether or not something is safe, we need a shared definition of what it is to be safe. If safety means free from all risk, then there is no safe activity. Just going to work you are exposed to traffic, street crime, contagious diseases, and all the stress-related illnesses that modern life incubates so efficiently.

A more workable definition of *safe* is "free of unacceptable risk," though one must then define what acceptable means, and that's different for different people at different times. *There is no objective truth about risk; there is just your truth.* If you like to base decisions on statistics, then I can tell you right now that it is safe to take a commercial flight, go to a ball game, visit a theme park. (In fact, major theme parks are about as safe as you can get. You are more likely to be injured driving there than being there.) If you base decisions solely on statistics, it's safe to tour the United Nations building while Yasir Arafat is giving a speech, or to travel to Israel — but that's not how most people determine their own level of acceptable risk.

Americans have always had strange ways of evaluating risk. We tend to give our full attention to risks that are beyond our control (earthquakes, mechanical failure on airplanes, nuclear-plant disasters) while ignoring those we feel in charge of (car accidents, disease from smoking, poor diet), even though the latter are far more likely to harm us. While we knowingly volunteer for some risks, we object to those imposed on us by others. We will tolerate familiar risks over strange ones. The hijacking of an American jet in Athens looms larger in our concern than the husband who kills his wife, even though one happens rarely, and the other happens every day (twelve times a day, in fact).

There are many Americans who wouldn't travel to see the Pyramids for fear of being killed in Egypt, so they stay home in Detroit where that danger is twenty times greater.

Sometimes, we can be absurdly risk-averse: After a fire on the Mir space station, I saw a TV news exposé proclaiming the space program unsafe for the astronauts. You mean sitting on the tip of a missile that's filled with rocket fuel and being blasted out of the atmosphere at 25,000 miles an hour is unsafe? Who'd have thought?

Risk assessment is part of life, just as risk itself is part of life. Military commanders measure the risk to troops before sending them into combat. Sometimes the stakes are so high that we are willing to accept great risk — as with the space program or the brave decision making that allowed U.S. soldiers to land on the beaches at Normandy on D day. Other times, we are unwilling to accept hardly any risk at all, as with the safety of our one-year-old child.

As our kids grow, however, we let them take greater risks: The tricycle gives way to the bicycle, which gives way to the motorcycle. The playdate becomes the sleepover, which becomes the camp, which becomes the camping trip. Our definition of acceptable risk expands to make room for life — and that's what we must do today: Redefine what constitutes acceptable risk, in order to make room for life.

The place to start is in your immediate environment. Look around right this moment, right where you are. I already know if you are reading this book, you are not in danger, for if you perceived danger — consciously or intuitively — you'd pause in your reading to assess it.

A central and major challenge to our natural defense system is that the reach of our perception in the satellite age has been extended way beyond the reach of that which might hurt us. For example, if you start where you are right now — in the room where you are sitting — all is well. Now extend in your imagination to the neighborhood and it's more difficult to know that all is well. If you keep widening the circle, you'll eventually get to Lantana, Florida, where a business received anthrax in the mail. Doesn't feel so safe anymore. Keep going, and you'll reach Milan, where there was an awful plane crash. Keep going and you'll reach Saudi Arabia and the shopping mall where a terrorist bomb killed two Americans.

In the satellite age, you see, we don't experience just the calamities in our own lives — we experience the calamities in everyone's life. So Americans have a far larger index of fears to draw upon.

Unwarranted fear will decrease when you reduce the size of the area in which you search for danger. Unwarranted fear will decrease further if you don't search for danger at all, but trust that intuition will come and get your attention if need be. More on that later.

An example of the way we evaluate risk and fear ties easily to the world of terrorism: In the 1960s there was a study done that sought to determine which single word has the greatest psychological impact on people. Researchers tested reactions to words such as *spider, snake, death, rape, incest, murder.* It was the word *shark* that elicited the greatest fear response (and this survey was before the book or movie *Jaws*). Why do sharks, which human beings come in contact with so rarely, frighten us so profoundly?

The seeming randomness of their strike is part of it, the lack of warning, the fact that such a large creature can approach silently and separate body from soul so dispassionately. To the shark, we are without identity, we are no more than meat, and for human beings the loss of identity is a type of death all by itself.

As with the shark attack, seeming randomness and lack of warning are the attributes of terroristic violence we fear most. Like sharks, some terrorists view us without identity; not as individuals but just as victims. Though there is no single strategy for avoiding terrorism, everything you need know to be safe from sharks can be spoken in five words: Don't go in the ocean. So perfect a precaution, and yet the overwhelming majority of people frolic in the waves, having determined the odds of a shark attack are acceptably low and trusting that if they receive a signal of danger they'll heed it. They have chosen to compartmentalize the reality of sharks — and to go on with life rather than remain in a state of fear.

Among many problems of remaining in a state of fear is that it can lead to panic, and panic itself is usually more dangerous than the outcome we dread. Rock climbers and long-distance ocean swimmers will tell you it isn't the mountain or the water that kills — it is panic.

Panic, the great enemy of survival, can be perceived as an unmanageable kaleidoscope of fears. It can be reduced through embracing the knowledge that what you fear is not happening. It might happen, to be sure, and that's why, in most instances, you get the signal in plenty of time to do something about it. From this point of view, true fear can actually be perceived as good news; since life has plenty of hazards that come upon us without warning, we could welcome fear with, "Thank God for a signal I can act on."

The wise words of FDR "The only thing we have to fear is fear itself" might be amended by nature: "There is nothing to fear unless and until you feel fear."

·   ·   ·

Just as some people are quick to predict the worst, there are others who are reluctant to accept that they might actually be in the presence of danger. This is often caused by the false belief that if we acknowledge risk we somehow invite or cause it to happen, and the opposite belief that if we don't acknowledge it, we prevent it from happening. Only human beings can look directly at something, have all the information they need to make an accurate prediction, perhaps even momentarily make the accurate prediction, and then say that it isn't so. But you have a choice about that.

To be freer of unwarranted fear and yet still get the gift of true fear, there are three goals to strive for. They aren't easy to reach, but I've found it to be worth trying:

1. When you feel fear or any intuitive signal, listen.
2. When you don't feel fear, don't manufacture it.
3. If you find yourself creating worry, explore and discover why.

Explore every intuitive signal, but briefly and not re-petitively. When faced with some worry or uncertain fear, ask yourself: Am I responding to something in my environment, or something in my imagination? Is this feeling based on something I perceive in my circumstance, or merely something in my memory? Is the fear that a terrorist will crash a plane into the Super Bowl based on the sight of a plane circling erratically over the stadium? Or is it based on the alarming words of that "security expert" I saw on the news this morning? Or a movie I saw more than a decade ago?

We all have the choice today to turn the frightening events we shared into something new and constructive: a life freer of unwarranted fear, and, believe it or not, a safer life than we had before September 11. Together, we have looked right at a truth more terrible than most of us had ever imagined, and we have prevailed, and in this experi-ence is the opportunity to look at fear itself differently.

When you honor intuitive signals and evaluate them without denial (believing that either the favorable or the unfavorable outcome is possible), you can actually relax, even in these troubled times. You need not be wary, for you will come to trust that you'll be notified if there is something worthy of your attention. Fear will gain credibility because it won't be applied wastefully. When you accept the survival signal as a welcome message and quickly evaluate your environment or situation, fear stops in an instant. Thus, *trusting intuition is the exact opposite of living in fear.* In fact, the role of fear in your life lessens as your mind and body come to know that you will listen to the quiet wind chime, and have no need for blaring sirens.

· 4 ·

BEING AN ANTI-TERRORIST:
The Messengers of Intuition

R ECALL THE STORY at the opening of the book
about the Nazi terrorist conspiracy foiled by the
FBI. The nation was motivated to act quickly, and six of
the conspirators were tried and sentenced to death within
weeks. A day after sentencing, all were electrocuted, and so
ended what was, for sixty years, America's worst-ever terrorist plot.

Because John Cullen listened to his intuition, our history is much different from what it might have been. It
also helped that the Nazi terrorists violated several rules of
effective conspiracy:

Don't let the operation get too big.
Be sure nobody knows all the players.
Discourage unneeded communication between
the cells.

Don't tell members anything they don't absolutely
   need to know.
Keep it simple.
Work only with pure devotees.
Don't draw attention.
Be patient.

Mohamed Atta and his associates broke fewer of these
rules.

When one compares the Nazi terrorist plan against
mainland America with current terrorist operations, the
main difference is the sophistication and availability of
technology. Otherwise, there are many instructive similari-
ties to learn from.

Though we were at war in 1942, most mainland Americans experienced the conflict in a distant way: primarily
through newsreels and journalistic reports. Similarly, even
though we have been at war with Middle Eastern terrorists
for many years now, until September 11 that war was distant to most Americans. The World Trade Center bombing in 1993, the bomb attack on the USS *Cole,* the hugely
destructive bombings of our embassies in Kenya and Tan-
zania, lethal attacks on U.S. servicemen overseas, including
one that killed 241 Marines — all this and more we were
able to ignore until September 11.

Much like today's terrorists, the Nazi terrorists planned
a decisive, dramatic event (scheduled for the Fourth of
July), to be followed by a long campaign of terror aimed at
alarming the population and destabilizing the economy.

Just as the 9/11 conspirators plotted something diabolical, the Nazi plan had dark and cruel components. Among the items they brought into America by submarine were explosives made to look like coal. Chunks were to be mixed in with the coal loaded onto trains, chunks that would explode when shoveled into the engines.

Much like the adversaries we now face, the Nazi terrorists were fanatics backed by millions of dollars in cash and resources and a network of support. Much like Mohamed Atta and his associates, the Nazi terrorists beheld a vulnerable, sleeping giant.

But today, that giant is not sleeping, and one of my objectives in this book is to offer ways to remain awake without remaining afraid.

THE NATURE OF SUSPICION

In the aftermath of September 11, you no doubt heard the many urgings of government officials to report anything suspicious to authorities. Most people, however, don't know precisely how to define *suspicious*.

Farrar Teeple, her father, and John Cullen all had the opportunity to become part of the national security — but only Cullen stayed the course and acted effectively. Teeple's father would surely have acted differently had he recognized what was right in front of him.

We deny because we're built to see what we want to see. In his book *The Day the Universe Changed,* historian James Burke points out that "It is the brain which sees, not the eye. Reality is in the brain before it is experienced, or else the signals we get from the eye would make no sense."

This truth underscores the value of having the pieces of the terroristic violence puzzle in our heads before we need them — and this chapter is committed to identifying many of those pieces.

Though FBI agents may recognize suspicious behaviors associated with conspiratorial violence, they are almost never in a position to see those behaviors. It is regular citizens who are watching the play as it unfolds, coming in contact with the characters, seeing pieces of the plot. Accordingly, the most effective way to detect and prevent terroristic conspiracies is for you and me to be part of an "All Eyes" approach to security.

As I explored in depth in *The Gift of Fear,* one of the most valuable elements of predicting and preventing violence is the pre-incident indicator, or PIN, as it's called in my firm. Pre-incident indicators occur prior to a final act of violence. As an example, let's look at the form of terrorism formerly most effective in America (often but not always committed by Americans): assassination. Imagine someone planning to assassinate a governor at a speech. Pre-incident indicators could include the assassin's jumping on stage with a gun — but that is too recent a PIN to be very useful (as it provides little time for intervention). The birth of the assassin is also a PIN, but it is too dated to be valuable. Even though both of these events are critical intersections on the map of this particular prediction, one hopes to be somewhere between the two, between the earliest detectable factor and those that occur an instant before the final act. Useful PINs for assassination might include the assassin's developing a plan, purchasing a weapon, keeping a diary, observing the governor in public, following him, trying to learn the governor's schedule, asking questions about his entry and exit points from a building, telling relatives "something big is coming," etc.

Preventing such attacks (which happens many times every year in America) requires understanding the process of this form of violence. Does an assassination attempt begin when the gun is fired at the target, or when the gun is drawn, or when it is carried secretly toward the stage, or when it is loaded, or when it is purchased, or when assassination is first thought of? We tend to focus too much on the end of incidents, and not enough on the process. Prediction moves from a science to an art when you realize that *pre-incident indicators are actually part of the incident.*

There are always PINs prior to violence, though they are not always recognized by those who see them.

In London, as a result of so many bombings by members of the IRA and others, residents are sensitive to PINs: An unattended suitcase leaning up against a building, a non-guest seen frequently in the lobby of a hotel, a pair of men climbing out from under a car belonging to a local politician — these things will quickly generate reports to law enforcement or security personnel. So it can be in America. If you intuit something questionable, ask questions — at least of yourself — and if the answers are unsatisfying, make a report to the police, the fire department, facility security, building management, or the FBI.

Since the willingness of regular citizens to report things

they perceive as suspicious will be a decisive element in detecting terrorist planning and logistics, let's start there, with the story of a young New Yorker named Andrew.

On the day his willingness was tested, he boarded the Lexington number 6 subway at around 8:00 A.M. and headed toward the Wall Street district for work. The car was packed with people, but one commuter stood out.

To Andrew, the man looked like he'd been living on the streets for some time, though he was more fit and younger than one expected a homeless person to be. He appeared agitated, maybe even a bit crazy — within the acceptable range of craziness one gets used to on the subway. He was wearing what looked like brand-new tennis shoes, white and clean — an odd match for his torn sweatshirt and tattered jeans. It wasn't his appearance that held Andrew's attention. It was the bulky canvas bag the man had placed on the floor between his feet, the strap of which he held firmly in both hands. The bag had been methodically covered with white surgical tape, leaving only its two wooden handles exposed. The handles themselves were interesting, firmly attached with thick chain, improvised to carry something heavy. The man would have earned less scrutiny but for a single word written boldly in dark blue marker across both sides of the stark white bag. The word was *BOMB*.

Andrew was not the only person who noticed this. He saw a few other passengers roll their eyes or exchange shrugs about the man and his unusual fashion statement. But nobody seemed too alarmed. People sat down next to the man, looked him over, and went back to reading their papers. They got off at their stops, and new people got on, looked him over, and opened up their papers.

Andrew got off the subway at Fulton Street, and so did that man. The pull of gravity kept the bag from swinging as he walked. *It is heavy,* Andrew thought as he watched the man labor his way up the stairs toward the street. Andrew turned left at the top of the stairs; the man and his precious bag went right and disappeared into the morning crowd.

Walking to his office, Andrew considered calling the police, but concluded that since nobody else seemed to be alarmed, maybe he shouldn't be either. That would have been the end of the story, except that sitting at his desk two hours later, Andrew heard an enormous explosion.

Co-workers rushed to the windows trying to see what was going on. After a while, unable to figure out what had happened, somebody got the idea to turn on the television. Soon enough they heard the words "We interrupt this program . . ."

Andrew focused intently on the video footage of people running away from what looked like a war zone. Some were bloodied, several were crying. Windows in all the surrounding buildings were blasted out. Smoke was everywhere. Ambulances and police cars sat in improvised parking spaces all over the street. The newsreader said estimates placed the number of injured at 150, "so it must have been a large bomb." Bomb. Andrew had ridden to work with that word.

When he told a couple of co-workers what he'd seen, they thought at first he was kidding. Maybe he shouldn't report it, he thought; the police might have the same reaction. Then he persuaded himself that someone on the subway must have already made the report, if not many people. The police were probably besieged by reports about that man.

Still, he decided to make the call, and after reaching a busy signal time and again, he was finally able to reach one of the detectives working on the case: "I'm sure plenty of people have already told you about the man on the subway with the bag marked *bomb*, but I thought I might have some details you could use. He was about thirty years —" The officer interrupted: "No, I haven't heard anything about that man, but it doesn't matter anyway, because we've solved that case."

Already solved? Andrew was impressed. Wanting to know if the mysterious man had been involved in the explosion, he asked if the officer could share some details of the crime.

"Sure. It turned out to be an explosion of a Mister Softee ice cream truck, a freak accident. No bomb." The officer chuckled. "But thanks for calling."

Even though the explosion near Andrew's office had turned out to be innocent, one might have hoped for more police curiosity about a man on the subway clinging to a canvas bag marked *bomb*. One might have hoped that at least a few of the thousands of people who encountered a man carrying a bag marked *bomb* would have called the police. But this happened in 1978. Today the story would be different.

When Andrew even momentarily thought that the

man on the subway might be linked to the huge explosion he heard, he could feel ridiculous — but in fact, it would have been more ridiculous to think anything else. Had that odd bag contained a bomb, a seemingly tiny detail from just one caller like Andrew might have attached to other fragments of evidence and led police to the prevention of more bombings. Thus, the exact same phone call could be seen either as a humorous distraction for a busy civil servant or as an admirable act. In our lives today, such a report is admirable either way.

If you have an intuitive feeling that something you've observed might be relevant to a crime (past or future), even if you can't fully explain why you feel what you feel, any effective, professional law-enforcement officer will want to hear about it and will welcome your report. If you encounter one who does not, his or her supervisor likely will.

Imagine three men rent the apartment upstairs and are always looking through binoculars at the nearby federal building. It could be nothing, but you feel suspicious. This is the point at which many observers assume they need to see more evidence in support of their suspicion. But here's the reality: That may be all you get — just a line of dialogue, not the whole play. The nature of conspiracy is that the elements of planning and logistics happen out of view of each other. You see one element.

Nobody shows up at the electronics store and asks for the bomb department, but you might encounter someone who asks for several bomb components in a row (timer, mercury switch, wire, battery, etc.). Your suspicion has to be enough, because if you wait to put what you've seen together with some decisive fact — such as the man buying explosives across town on the same day — you'll miss the opportunity intuition is telling you about.

You don't have to build the entire criminal conspiracy case. You need only honor what you feel, observe what you can, document information, and make the call.

Suspicion has gotten a bad name for some reason; people feel guilty about it. But when you feel suspicious, it's not something unkind that you're doing to someone; it's not something you choose — suspicion is something that chooses you. You don't feel guilty when curiosity arises, and suspicion, like curiosity, is just a messenger of intuition. Suspicion is curiosity with the added intuitive instruction to keep watching. In fact, the root of the word *suspicion* — *suspicere* — means "to watch."

If you make a report and it turns out there was no hazard, you have lost nothing and you've added a new distinction to your intuition, so that it might not sound the alarm again in the same situation. Intuition is always learning, and though it may occasionally send a signal that turns out to be less than urgent, everything it communicates to you has meaning. When you get an intuitive signal, most of the work is already done — your conscious job is to search for the meaning and, even if you don't initially find it, to believe it might be there nonetheless. Unlike worry, intuition will not waste your time; it is always in response to something, and always has your best interest at heart.

If you make a report, you cannot be wrong. In fact, in this context — and in this time — I'd propose a new definition of *wrong:* You can be wrong only if you deny your intuition and don't put a higher value on safety than you put on pride.

THE MESSENGERS OF INTUITION

Intuition might send any of several messengers to get your attention, and because they differ according to urgency, it is good to know the ranking. The intuitive signal of the highest order is fear. The next level is apprehension, then suspicion, then hesitation, doubt, gut feelings, hunches, and curiosity. There are also nagging feelings, persistent thoughts, physical sensations, wonder, and anxiety. Generally speaking, these are less urgent.

THE MESSENGERS OF INTUITION

Nagging feelings
Persistent thoughts
Humor
Wonder
Anxiety
Curiosity
Hunches
Gut feelings
Doubt
Hesitation
Suspicion
Apprehension
Fear

You may be surprised to see humor as a signal of intuition.

In one story that offers an excellent example, all the information was there like a great unharvested crop left to dry in the sun. The receptionist was off that day, so Bob Taylor and others at the California Forestry Association sorted through the mail. When they came upon the package, they looked it over and chatted about what to do with it. It was addressed to the former president of the association, and they debated whether to just forward it to him. When Gilbert Murray, the current president, arrived, they brought him in on their discussion. Murray said, "Let's open it."

Taylor got up and cracked a joke: "I'm going back to my office before the bomb goes off." He walked down the hall to his desk, but before he sat down, he heard the enormous explosion that killed his boss. Because of intuition, that bomb didn't kill Bob Taylor.

All the information he needed was there and dismissed by the others, but not before Taylor's intuition sent a signal to everyone in the clearest language: "I'm going back to my office before the bomb goes off."

Humor, particularly dark humor, is a common way to communicate concern without the risk of feeling silly afterward, and without overtly showing fear. But how does this type of remark evolve? One doesn't consciously direct the mind to search all files for something funny to say. Were that the case, Bob Taylor might have looked at this package addressed to a man who didn't work there anymore and cleverly said, "It's probably a fruitcake that's been lost in the mail since Christmas," or any of thousands of comments. Or he could have made no comment at all. But with this type of humor, an idea comes into consciousness that, in context, seems so outlandish as to be ridiculous. And that's precisely why it's funny. The point is, though, that the idea came into consciousness because all the information was there.

That package sent by the Unabomber to the California Forestry Association was very heavy. It was covered with tape, had too much postage, and aroused enough interest that several people speculated on whether it might be a bomb. They had noted the Oakland firm named on the return address — had they called directory assistance, they'd have found it to be fictitious. Still, it was opened.

A few weeks earlier, advertising executive Thomas Mosser received such a package at his New Jersey home. Just before he opened it, something made him curious (a messenger of intuition), and he asked his wife if she was expecting a parcel at the house. She said she was not. Mosser had asked a good question, but a moment later he ignored the answer he'd sought. He was killed when he opened the package (also sent by the Unabomber).

Postal inspector Dan Mihalko: "I've heard many times that people would make a comment, 'This looks like a bomb,' and still open it. That's one for the psychologists to answer. Perhaps they don't want to call the police and be embarrassed if it turns out to be nothing."

The Unabomber himself mocked some of the twenty-three targets hurt by his bombs: "If you had any brains you would have realized that there are a lot of people out there who resent the way techno-nerds like you are changing the world and you wouldn't have been dumb enough to open an unexpected package from an unknown source. People with advanced degrees aren't as smart as they think they are."

In fairness to the victims discussed above, mail bombs are very rare and were not the type of hazard one was normally concerned about, but the point is that these victims were concerned enough to comment on it. Though you've likely never had reason to think about mail bombs, they are now on the menu of terroristic options — and now part of your intuition.

Intuition is knowing without knowing why, knowing even when you can't see the evidence. Denial is choosing not to know something even when the evidence is obvious. It's easy to see which of these two human abilities is more likely to protect us during challenging times.

But what about ordinary times? Here's Bill McKenna's story of an intuitive signal that tried to warn him of a burglary: "As I was dozing off I heard a noise downstairs which for some reason really scared me. It wasn't that it was loud, and I don't even recall exactly what it sounded like, but I absolutely couldn't shake it. So I got out of bed and went downstairs to be sure everything was all right. I made a quick walk around and then went back to bed. Half an hour later, I heard a sound so quiet that I still don't know how it woke me; it was the sound of someone else's breathing. I turned on the light, and there was this burglar standing in the middle of the room with our CD player under his arm."

If Bill's mission on his walk downstairs was "to be sure everything was all right," as he put it, then he succeeded completely. If, though, it was to answer the survival signal — to accept the gift of fear — he failed. When he heard that noise downstairs, had he consciously linked the fear he felt to its possible dangerous outcomes — as his intuition had already done — he might have conducted his search with the goal of finding risk as opposed to the goal of finding nothing. Had he thought, in effect, "Since I feel fear, I know there is some reason, so what is it?" then he could have brought into consciousness what his intuition already knew and what he remembered and later told me: The living-room light had been on when he got home, the cat had somehow gotten outside and was waiting on the porch, an unusual old car was parked near his driveway, its engine clinking as it cooled.

Even more common than burglary is just occasional fear of another person. Imagine a woman waiting for an elevator. When the doors open she sees a man inside who causes her to feel fear. Since she is not usually afraid, it may be the late hour, his size, the way he looks at her, the rate of attacks in the neighborhood, an article she read a year ago — it doesn't matter why. The point is, she feels fear. How does she respond to nature's strongest survival signal? She suppresses it, telling herself: "I'm not going to insult this guy by letting the door close in his face." When the fear doesn't go away, she tells herself not to be so silly, and she gets into the elevator.

Now, which is sillier: waiting a moment for the next elevator, or getting into a soundproof steel chamber with a stranger she is afraid of? The same question now applies to any of us faced with something that we feel, even for a fleeting moment, might be worth exploring further or reporting to law enforcement.

Just as intuition protects us from danger, denial protects us from something, too: unwelcome information. Denial serves to eliminate the discomfort of accepting realities we'd rather not acknowledge. There are times this protection is valuable for emotional survival, but it is rarely useful for physical survival — and these days, it's downright destructive to the safety of the nation. Like intuition, denial sends signals you can recognize. When you detect these cues at work in yourself, you can stop and ask one of life's most powerful questions: "What am I choosing not to see here?"

THE SIGNALS OF DENIAL

Rationalization
Justification
Minimization
Excuse-making
Refusal

Recall that scenario in which three men rent the apartment upstairs and spend all their time looking through binoculars at the nearby federal building.

You could acknowledge the suspiciousness of that circumstance, or you could tell yourself, "They're probably architecture students" (rationalization); "Hey, they're allowed to do what they want, they're not hurting anybody" (justification); "They're just looking, that's all" (minimization); "It's not my responsibility to watch everybody" (excuse-making); "I'm not going to be the kind of person who's suspicious of everyone" (refusal).

We only minimize that which looms large, and the fact that we make an excuse for one of our choices is often a sign that we perceive something wrong with that choice.

Can you imagine an animal reacting to an intuitive signal the way some people do, with disdain and debate instead of attention? No animal in the wild suddenly overcome with fear would spend any of its mental energy thinking, "It's probably nothing." Too often we chide ourselves for even momentarily giving validity to the feeling that someone's unusual behavior might be sinister. Instead of being grateful for having a powerful internal resource, instead of entertaining the possibility that our minds might actually be working for us and not just playing tricks on us, we rush to ridicule the impulse. We, in contrast to every other creature in nature, choose not to explore — and even choose to ignore — survival signals. The mental energy we use searching for the innocent explanation to everything can today be more constructively applied to our shared national security.

Some people as much as refuse to accept our present situation. "I don't want to be looking at everyone suspiciously," one man said to me recently. Actually, if you listen to intuition, that will not happen. We intuitively trust people so often that we barely even notice it. The salesperson, the new neighbor, the friend of a friend, the secretary at the tax accountant's office, the guy who towed the car, the couple next to us at the movie theater — we automatically assessed each of them, felt no hesitation, and that was that.

Assessing the routine behavior of people is so simple, in fact, that we rarely even bother to do it consciously. We react only to the unusual. The man next to us on the plane for five hours garners little of our attention until, out of the corner of one eye, we see that he is reading the magazine in our hand. The point is that we intuitively evaluate people all the time, quite attentively, but they get our conscious attention only when there is a reason. We see it all, but we edit out most of it.

Since the overwhelming majority of people we encounter are not behaving suspiciously, that is just what our intuition correctly concludes virtually all of the time. Accordingly, on those rare occasions when we are suspicious about someone, it's worth asking ourselves why.

BEING AN ANTI-TERRORIST:
The Architecture of Conspiracy

The security of our nation and industries requires
the participation of government, business, our
citizens, and other nations of the world having
similar values as our own.

— SIR JOHN A. MACDONALD (1867)

WE'VE DISCUSSED SEVERAL of the reasons people
might override an intuitive signal: the concern
about being embarrassed by making a report that turns out
to be unimportant, reluctance to honor one's own intuition, and refusal to accept that the nation is at war with
extremists. There's a final reason someone might ignore a
PIN they feel could be relevant to terrorism: People are
understandably reluctant to acknowledge that they might
be in the presence of a person who could commit some
terrible violence.

And yet so many Americans have had to admit in retrospect that they were in the presence of our nation's most
prolific mass killers. Despite the fact that Mohamed Atta
and his associates moved around often and intentionally
avoided mingling with Americans, they were surprisingly
well remembered by a diverse group of people.

For example, Robert Solberg lived in an apartment complex where two of the 9/11 terrorists (Alhazmi and Al-Midhar) rented an apartment. He and other neighbors saw the men frequently, often carrying briefcases and speaking on cell phones. "Everybody around their apartment said they never had the lights on downstairs and didn't seem to have a regular phone," Solberg recalls. "But they weren't that noticeable." And yet he did notice.

Often people will say about some particular detail, "I realize this now, but I didn't know it then." Of course, if it is in their heads now, so was it then. What they mean is that only in retrospect do they recognize the significance of a given detail. My point is not that Robert Solberg should have made a police report, but rather that people in that apartment complex registered things they observed. That happens only when the mind perceives that something is worth placing into retrievable memory.

Much of what people remember about Mohamed Atta and his associates could have value to your intuition.

For example, they almost always moved around in pairs and they had little luggage, often using plastic bags to transport their few belongings. At one apartment, on the ground floor they had no furniture. Often they did not have telephone service and relied upon cell phones. Perhaps most observable: *They were busy, had money, and yet obviously did not have jobs.* (All of these same PINs could apply to other types of conspiratorial criminals as well.)

Ed Murray, who lived in the same apartment building as two of the terrorists, saw them playing flight-simulator games late at night. He noted how busy they were: "Anytime you saw them, they were on their cell phones." Another neighbor, Nancy Coker, saw them getting into limousines on several different nights, even though they had a car of their own. "In this neighborhood," she said, "you notice stuff like that."

Would any of this persuade an observer to conclude that these men were about to become murderers? No, but much of it is enough to stimulate curiosity, more questions, a discussion with other neighbors, and perhaps — when these steps don't quiet intuition, when suspicion increases instead of abates — a police report.

Although the soon-to-be hijackers unhesitatingly paid thousands of dollars for lessons while training at Huffman Flight School, they leased a room in the home of a bookkeeper at the school for just seventeen dollars a night.

It's clear that some of the 9/11 hijackers drew attention just by virtue of being foreigners who did not speak English well, and that's natural. It is also natural that Americans today scrutinize Middle Eastern men in ways they might not have prior to September 11. That will be true for a while, and then it will pass because we'll all have enough experiences with Middle Eastern visitors whom we don't link to terrorism. Still, while it may be politically correct to ignore a group of young, fit Middle Eastern men who board a flight and sit wordlessly in first class, people won't ignore them. Ethnicity may be what draws your attention to someone, and in the context of terrorism, it is neither entirely relevant nor entirely irrelevant — but behavior is what will most inform your intuition.

For example, about two weeks before September 11,

Marwan Al-Shehhi and another man checked into the Panther Motel in Deerfield Beach, Florida. They paid $500 in advance. One of the owners of the motel, Richard Surma, noticed that the men didn't go to the nearby beach. His wife, Diane, noticed that they used a towel to cover a picture on the wall in their room, a picture of a woman whose dress exposed one shoulder.

After they checked out on September 9, a box-cutter knife was found in their room, and several things were found in the trash they left behind: illustrated books on karate and jujitsu, FAA air-traffic maps, information on flying Boeing passenger jets, and fifty training textbooks. These items assume now a dark meaning to us that they did not have for Richard Surma back then, and yet he kept the items he found in their trash. When he and his wife heard Peter Jennings report that some of the terrorists had been in Florida and had taken flight lessons, intuition made all the connections, and the Surmas called the police.

What if there's nothing suspicious about any of the encounters people might have with future terrorist conspirators?

Well, sometimes there isn't much that's suspicious — but some of the time there will be, and it might be just one person from one encounter who makes one report that gets law enforcement to knock on one door to ask some questions. And it might be the right door. Imagine that sheriff's investigators had followed up on reports they'd received, and knocked on the door at Eric Harris's house in the days prior to his mass shooting at Columbine High School. Imagine that they'd asked, "Mind if we look around?" That question might have led to the discovery of some of the weapons and bombs.

Atta and his comrades were trying to live by the terrorist handbook that had served many of their predecessors well: "When you're in the outer world, you have to act like them, dress like them, behave like them." But they just couldn't pull it off.

For example, more than one librarian around the country reported later on members of the 9/11 conspiracy used public library computers in the weeks before the crime — presumably for e-mail and research. In Delray Beach, Florida, librarian Kathleen Hensman said three of the hijackers monitored her to make sure she couldn't see what they were doing online. She said to a colleague at the time, "What's their problem? I don't have a problem with them; why are they looking at me?" She remembers this because their behavior stood out.

When behaviors draw our attention, make us curious, lead us to wonder — that's intuition speaking. What you observe may turn out to be no problem at all, for many signals from intuition are merely requests that you keep perceiving to see if there's anything there worth being more concerned about. That's precisely what Kathleen Hensman was doing when the secretive visitors doubled their efforts to ensure she couldn't observe what they were up to.

Library staff see strangers all the time, so the issue here isn't strangers; the issue is *strangeness*.

■   ■   ■

The terrorist weapon that has proved most consistently reliable is the bomb, perhaps because it meets two important criteria of terror: destructiveness and provocation of fear. To apply some of what we've explored thus far, let's look at an imaginary case study: Three men have decided to build, deliver, and detonate a series of large bombs.

To accomplish that, they need technical skill or information, money, explosives components, a triggering mechanism, a private place to assemble the deadly device, a way to get items from the car into the assembly area while remaining out of view, a way to secure the location when it's not attended (they can't afford a burglary attempt in which someone sees what they are doing), a truck for delivering their devices, a way to get completed bombs from the assembly location to the vehicle, and so on.

First of all, are they fated to succeed? Of course not.

John Kennedy promoted a myth in America when he remarked that assassins could not be stopped because "all anyone has to do is be willing to trade his life for the President's." Kennedy's oft-quoted opinion is glib, but entirely wrong. In fact, assassination not only can be prevented but is prevented far more often than is successful. And the same is true for other forms of terrorism. Bomb components are found and confiscated (as happened not long ago at a Philadelphia train station), informants come forward, police surveillance pays off and leads to arrests, intelligence analysts see patterns that lead to intervention, the National Security Agency overhears a conversation and uses the information to foil an assassination attempt (as happened when U.S. intelligence intercepted information about a plot to kill former President George Bush and former Secretary of State James Baker during their visit to Kuwait shortly after they left office), and terrorists building explosives have accidents that end plots permanently.

Indeed, people aspiring to bold, dramatic acts have some advantages over their victims, but there are many more factors working against them. Literally thousands of opportunities exist for them to fail, and only one slender opportunity exists for them to succeed. Assassination, for example, is not the type of crime a person can practice — both literally and figuratively, an assassin has one shot at success.

Conspirators who want to be able to commit more than one act have the extra complication of needing to accomplish all this without being subsequently traceable. Let's make that the case with the three men planning to detonate bombs. Now, the truck and much of what they buy has to be obtained in an unconventional way. Finally, on the day of placement, bombs must be delivered in total secrecy, out of the view of potential witnesses and video cameras — not to mention security personnel and police.

While any of us might observe some element of this plot and then report useful information to law enforcement, people working in particular industries are more likely to get that opportunity.

For example, a business that sells farming supplies, including ammonium nitrate fertilizer and agricultural chemicals, is one of the places likely to encounter someone trying to obtain materials for building a bomb. (Ammonium nitrate is what Timothy McVeigh used so effectively to injure and kill hundreds of people at the Oklahoma City federal building.)

Though only a few readers of this book will be in the farming-supplies business, this example contains useful information about the thought processes that lead to suspicion.

A proprietor of such a business knows the farmers in his area well; he knows the farms, the soil, the crops. So when a new customer arrives to purchase ammonium nitrate, there might be any number of things that trigger intuition:

- a customer's resistance to consider any other product
- lack of familiarity with farming (can't knowledgeably answer questions about acreage, crops, soil composition, etc.)
- a desire to take the product right away, with no interest in delivery
- payment in cash
- impatient, nervous, uncommunicative behavior

An encounter with someone like this could stimulate a proprietor to begin mentally noting the visitor's appearance, descriptive information about his vehicle, and other features of the situation. Is the customer alone? The encounter might also stimulate the proprietor to ask more questions. How long has he been in farming? Where's his property? Is he willing to be on the firm's mailing list? If suspicion survives this process, the proprietor could retain any paper or items the visitor touched (for fingerprints and other evidentiary use) and call the authorities (in this instance the Bureau of Alcohol, Tobacco and Firearms, at 1-800-800-3855, twenty-four hours a day).

Most of us assume that our own businesses would not likely encounter conspiratorial criminals, but plots can touch many people. For example, our hypothetical bombers would also need a remote rental property somewhere, a place where they can work and be absolutely certain that nobody could see what they're doing — so this would bring them into contact with Realtors, property owners, managers, nearby residents, other tenants. Their need for furniture would bring them to businesses that sell or rent it. Like any tenant, they'd need the utilities turned on, which would require some paperwork, a payment method, and an identity. They may already have cellular phones, but if the property is remote, they might need regular phone service as well.

Why don't they just steal everything they need? They could, and some terrorist organizations in the world have subgroups with no mission other than to rob banks — just as a way to get cash. But theft greatly increases the likelihood of getting caught, and our group wants to be able to strike more than once. Further, a theft becomes an operation all its own — and uses up the resources of planning. It may save money, but it can cost invisibility.

Solely for the purposes of stimulating your thinking and with no expectation of producing a comprehensive list, here are a few of the service and product providers that our team of aspiring serial bombers or other terrorists might encounter, along with some of the reasons why:

Property ownership, management, and representation
Rentals at remote locations, warehouses, storage buildings, small industrial facilities

Fertilizer manufacturing and/or sale
Ingredients for bombs

Library
Research information, access to the Internet

Electronics stores and catalogs
Wire, timers, switches, mini-batteries, etc. (Radio Shack has been the store of choice for many clandestine device makers.)

Banking
Credit cards for purchases through the mail or over the Internet

Department of Motor Vehicles
Identification, false identification

Hall of Records, Passport Office
Identification, false identification

Utilities
Electricity, gas, phone service

Car sales or rental
Vehicles

Truck sales or rental
Learning about trucks, choosing one, obtaining one

Pool supply and chemical sales
Chlorine

Private airports
Access to small aircraft, or adjacent major airports

Air-conditioning repair
Knowledge about ventilation systems, access to
    particular sites

Security systems
Knowledge about security systems, information on
    specific protected sites

Security services
Guard uniforms, credentials, access to records

Transportation
Tanker trucks, trucks already containing dangerous
    material

Hardware store
Tools

Hobby shops and catalogs
Radio remote-control equipment

Mail and express carriers (UPS, FedEx)
Sending hazardous packages, explosive devices, etc.

Gun store, gun shows
Weapons, gunpowder, weapons components

Fireworks sales
Black powder, explosives materials

Construction, commercial storage, military bases, mining operations
Explosives

Bookstores
Research

Conspiracy helps us see more clearly that violence is a process — and that's true regardless of whether it's committed by individuals, teams, organizations, or even nations. Though news reports often say about an act of American-style terrorism, such as an assassination or a multiple shooting, that the perpetrator "just snapped," it never, ever happens.

There is a process as observable, and often as predictable, as water coming to a boil. Though reports are quick to give some expression of violence a name, such as calling something an act of "school violence," it is really every type of violence, committed by every type of perpetrator, with many types of motives. A school shooting might be a revenge killing, when a student who feels humiliated or emasculated proves that he cannot be taken lightly. It might be relationship violence, when a student shoots his ex-girlfriend. It might be date stalking, when the young man who refuses to let go attacks his victim in her classroom. It might be rage killing, when a student primed to do something big and bad chooses to do it at his school.

Fortunately, violence of any kind offers many predictive opportunities, and there are almost always several people in a position to observe the warning signs. We know that obvious warnings are frequently ignored, but we also know that it doesn't have to be that way.

To pull all the information in this chapter together, I'm offering several examples below. You might or might not encounter these specific behaviors, but they are the kind of observations often relevant to conspiratorial crimes. The concepts will remain forever in your intuition, just because you read them once.

- As you arrive at work one morning, two men in their late forties ask you how they might get onto the roof of a nearby warehouse. When you ask why, they explain that they want to take photographs of planes taking off and landing at the adjacent airport. They say it's for "a school project."

- You see a man at the mall hurry away after putting down a heavy-looking suitcase.
- A new neighbor arrives home late one night wearing a police uniform — and you don't recall his being a cop.
- You work at a gun store and two foreign nationals visit several times asking about high-powered rifles. One of them asks lots of questions about how to modify the rifle so that it's fully automatic. To make their purchase, they put down five hundred-dollar bills, but when you give them a form to fill out, they storm out of the store, complaining that you have too much paperwork.
- You work in the City Hall records room. You get a voice mail asking that you fax the caller copies of the building's architectural plans. Later, another man calls and makes the same request. When you advise him that an in-person request is necessary, he hangs up.
- You work the late shift at a power plant. One night you get a call from someone identifying himself as a police investigator. He wants to speak to you about "an important case" and asks that you arrange a pass for him at the gate, which you do. He never shows up and you don't hear from him again. You decide to call the security gate to see if someone entered using the pass you arranged. The answer turns out to be yes.

In the last two examples, there is evidence likely to be of value: the fax number given by the first caller asking for building plans, and the record (or maybe even videotape) of the vehicle that entered using the pass you arranged.

I've presented a lot of information and examples in this chapter. Retaining the specifics in your memory is not important, because your intuition will do most of the work.

Ultimately, no matter how well you do your part in listening to an intuition about suspicious behavior, you'll need to have faith that the police will do theirs. But you decide where to invest your faith, and you must invest some of it in yourself. That may mean being willing to act even when it's inconvenient, unpopular, or downright rude. For example, can you imagine insisting that a police officer take a report he seems reluctant to pursue? I hope you can. Can you imagine calling an officer's supervisor if you feel it's necessary? I hope you can.

You might also wonder if law-enforcement agencies and government are able to react to information from the public in ways that make a difference. After all, some would ask, "The FBI and the CIA got plenty of pre-incident indicators before September eleventh, and didn't they fail miserably?"

The short answer is no, they didn't fail miserably, particularly given the factors at play before September 11. I'll address the role of the FBI and the intelligence agencies in detail later on, but for now, be assured that a slight suspicion, a curiosity, a lingering thought, or a nagging feeling that you convert into further scrutiny can make — and every day does make — an enormous difference to our safety. Certainly there are improvements to be made in law enforcement and intelligence, and many are under way. One of the most effective is in your hands, however, and as more of us participate, our collective anti-terrorist determination becomes a surveillance system with a hundred million unique views of America.

"ANYONE MIGHT BE A TERRORIST"
"TERRORISTS ARE EVERYWHERE"
"REMAIN ALERT AT ALL TIMES"
"THE DANGER IS ALL AROUND US"

News reports and government officials have encouraged us to be "extra alert" or vigilant. I am not suggesting this at all, for I believe that when your defense system is properly informed, it is on duty whether or not you are alert. Alertly looking around while thinking, "Someone could jump out from behind *that* hedge; maybe there's someone hiding in *that* car," replaces perception of what is actually happening with imaginings of what could happen. This is limiting. We are far more open to all signals when we don't focus on the expectation of specific signals.

I do not propose that you look for terrorists. First of all, it's not true that "anybody might be a terrorist." Your daughter's drama teacher is not a terrorist; your best friend is not a terrorist; your tax accountant is not a terrorist. Second, the concept that "they" are everywhere not only is inaccurate but quickly loses credibility. Imagine being told, "The way to get rich is this: every place you go, look for a bag of diamonds." For a time, your brain would look for the diamonds, and then, never having found them, it would stop. Rather than looking for diamonds — which are rare — you could more constructively look for opportunities. In the context of terrorism, rather than looking for obvious terrorists — who are rare — be open to your own curiosity and suspicion, which are not so rare.

The warning to "remain alert!" is presumably said toward the goal of making it more difficult for terrorists to operate in America — but it may have the opposite effect. That's because it's not possible to remain at the highest level of alertness beyond a short period of time. Consider the people guarding the airports. They looked sharp and keen at the start of their new assignments — on the lookout — but less so every day. Now you see them chatting, laughing, leaning against things, etc.

That's because the much-anticipated terrorist attack takes its time (intentionally), and after a while things you once felt were suspicious prove time and again to be normal, then routine, then even boring.

Alertness is one of nature's temporary triggered states; it is in response to something, and when that something fades, so does the alertness. To maintain it artificially is possible — Secret Service agents and people from my firm's Protective Security Division have to do it — but it is an acquired skill, not a natural ability. And it is a skill you don't need in order to accomplish the specific recommendation I offer: Get back to normal life, deny less, honor your intuition more, and be willing to make a report if life places something relevant to terrorism in your view.

If you and enough others agree with and embrace this

recommendation, it will make ours a nation safer from all forms of crime and violence — not just terrorism, but also homicide, femicide, drug dealing, burglary, robbery, domestic violence, child abuse, and so many other behaviors that cause us pain and erode the quality of our lives. This is a process I believe has started and has already made America safer today for most citizens than it was on September 10.

· 6 ·

APOCALYPSE NOT NOW

What we're talking about is getting to know fear,
becoming familiar with fear, looking it right in
the eye — not as a way to solve problems, but as a
complete undoing of old ways of seeing, hearing,
smelling, tasting and thinking.

— Pema Chodron Shambhala
Author, *When Things Fall Apart*

WHAT'S THE BOTTOM LINE?" people often ask me. "Will terrorists detonate a nuclear bomb? Spread smallpox? Release nerve gas? What's the worst-case scenario?"

You have probably known someone who experienced a trauma, then later seen that person reliving the tragedy. There is also such a thing as *pre-living* a tragedy. Exactly as we benefit from letting go of the past, millions of Americans will benefit from letting go of the worst-case future. Someone proposes a so-called worst-case scenario (as if there could be any objective view of what would constitute the worst case), and then the scenario gets discussed so much on television that it comes to seem like it's about to happen.

A worst-case scenario is a theoretical sequence of events intentionally devised to be as bad as possible, the word *scenario* coming from *scene,* as in a scene in a play or movie. Worst-case scenarios are creative exercises, not predictions of likely events. If we had examples of the realities to explore, we'd be doing that, but in most instances, we have only the imagination to chew on. Remember, these things enter the stream of discussion specifically because they are not likely, specifically because they are at the far end of possibility, and specifically because they have not ever happened.

These things start with someone saying, "Geez, what if terrorists got hold of an intercontinental ballistic missile?" Then TV news personalities interview experts in some loosely related field, a scary graphic is developed (say, a mushroom cloud emerging from the top of a local playground), then they hound a government official with the question "But isn't it possible that someone could get hold of an intercontinental ballistic missile?" and he says how unlikely that is, but acknowledges that it is possible (i.e., within the realm of physics and imagination) — and we're off and running.

The human mind pounces on this sort of thing because it can seem relevant to survival. We're hard-wired to entertain every thought of danger that's put in front of us, to turn it over, to look at it from every angle. The more enormous a lethal danger might be and the more people it might harm, the more fascinating it is. But for us to be fascinated by something, it has to be made accessible to our minds. For example, Earth coming out of its orbit and spinning off into a collision with Jupiter is too hard for us to get our minds around, but the idea of someone using a makeshift nuclear bomb has been made to appear plausible simply because of so much discussion.

Though TV news carries theoretical discussions of doom further than other media, magazines and newspapers do their part. Journalists are writers, and they love creative stories, so we get detailed accounts of precisely how terrible a terrible outcome could be. Editors love a dramatic hook, and you're the fish they're trying to catch with it. Print may seem to give credibility to worst-case scenarios, but the truth is that only you decide what credibility to invest in any given doomsday tale.

You've probably heard that anyone can easily get information about how to build a nuclear bomb by just logging on to the Internet. Have you tried "just logging on to the Internet" and getting those simple step-by-step instructions? Do you know how to build a nuclear bomb? Whenever I hear about how easy it is, I am reminded of an old routine from the brilliant humorist, author, and filmmaker Steve Martin: He would promise to tell his audience the secret of how one could earn a million dollars and yet pay absolutely *no* taxes. "First," he'd say as if this were the easy part, "earn a million dollars." To all those who make nuclear-bomb construction sound as simple as putting up Christmas lights, I'd say, "First, get some plutonium or highly enriched uranium."

Someday some person or group may indeed detonate a small nuclear device somewhere on earth. It will be awful. It will harm some people. It will be recovered from. After we accept that it could happen, is it constructive to spend every day between now and then trying to experience the event in our minds?

The future is longer than the past, and because the future occurs on the foundation of the past, more will happen than has happened. This means that nearly everything we can imagine has some likelihood of happening sometime, particularly if you include far-off times. In a truly intelligent worst-case scenario, one would theorize that some young Americans bent on grand mischief are far more dangerous than foreign terrorists. They are here, they are brilliant, some are reckless, some are homicidal and suicidal; and we must assume that the extraordinary knowledge being accumulated in our society and made available to young people will be misused. Many teenagers are capable of mounting ferocious attacks and many have the motivation to do so — as we have learned from tragedies like Columbine. What a thirty-year-old would find discouragingly difficult to accomplish, an eighteen-year-old will keep trying. What a thirty-year-old might find too reckless or dangerous, an eighteen-year-old might find intriguing.

I make this point to bring some perspective during a time when Americans have focused almost entirely on Middle Eastern terrorists. When anthrax spores were sent through the mail after 9/11, we were fascinated to know if the crime was linked to the attack on the World Trade Center. This raises one of the most salient questions about risk: *Does motive matter?* It's understandable that people are more afraid if anthrax spores are sent by Middle Eastern terrorists, even though there are far more American-bred attention-seekers who might do this kind of thing. Excessive fascination with motive and with the origins of risk can cloud our ability to make an effective assessment of what is really likely and how to respond to events that actually occur. Whether sent by an American or a Middle Easterner, the best management of the anthrax cases remains the same.

There are people whose jobs require some degree of worst-case thinking. I am one of them. Whole teams of threat-assessment practitioners in my firm spend their time developing contingency plans and responses to cover a variety of unfavorable outcomes. For example, making arrangements for a controversial public figure to give a speech at a rally about an emotionally charged political issue calls for contingency plans about many kinds of things that could happen, but we put more effort into those possibilities that are most likely.

An assassin in the audience, at the vehicle-arrival area, or along the foot route from the car to the holding room; a sniper in the distance; a bomb that was placed a week before the event; someone trying to strike the public figure; even a pie attack — all these things and more are on our list during the days of planning leading up to such an appearance. I do not oppose contingency planning. I do oppose time wasting, however, and in my firm, in my life, and in your life, everything we give energy to takes energy away from something else. Accordingly, we are wisest to put our resources where they'll be most likely to return some benefit.

You already live your life according to that equation, deciding where to put your protective resources at home, for example. Though intruders could land a helicopter on your roof and core through the ceiling, you've decided that entry via the front door is more likely — and you've got a lock that requires a key. A criminal could photograph your credit cards with a telephoto lens and then painstakingly duplicate them, but you've determined that someone taking your purse is more likely — so you watch it carefully. If there's an emergency phone list in your home, the names and numbers reflect your family's assessment of likely hazards. Is the U.S. Department of Energy Nuclear Emergency Search Team on that list? Probably not, and you're not likely to need that phone number. You also have a list in your head of things you want to avoid or prevent. You base the list on experience, logic, new information, and intuition. The list has limits — *because it has to*.

Conversely, worst-case scenarios have no limits. Wherever the imagination can travel, your mind can take you there. But the trip is voluntary — even when TV news producers are urging you to go, you don't have to.

Three terrible possibilities in particular have dominated the national dialogue: chemical, biological, and nuclear attacks. Normally, it's fair to assume that when everybody is discussing something, it's likely to happen, but that equation is warped a bit by people on television news shows — who will discuss anything.

In 1997, then-Secretary of Defense William Cohen appeared on an ABC News show and held up a five-pound bag of sugar, threatening that "This amount of anthrax could be spread over a city — let's say the size of Washington. It would destroy at least half the population of that city. If you had even more amounts —" Let me interrupt Mr. Cohen for a moment and recall that he also said, "One small particle of anthrax would produce death within five days." With that kind of inaccurate ad-fear-tising, it's no surprise that every scenario we used to hear about anthrax involved the death of hundreds of thousands or even "millions, millions," as Cohen was intoning when interviewer Cokie Roberts actually said to him, "Would you put that bag down, please." We have had several instructive examples of how worst-case scenarios fail to follow the creative scripts people write. For example, since the dread begun by Cohen's bag-of-sugar threat, we've actually experienced some biological attacks — and they've been far different from the scenarios we were offered.

Before 2001, did you ever hear a scenario about anthrax that went like this?

Somebody will put anthrax spores in letters and send them around several East Coast cities. Fewer than one hundred people will be exposed to the bacteria, and about thirty will get sick and be successfully treated. A few will die. There will be absolutely no impact on the health of 280 million other Americans, though the events will cause sadness and fear around the nation. In a city the size of Washington, D.C., fewer people will die from anthrax than from bites and bee stings.

So, anthrax has gone from a mass killer that would leave nobody alive to even write a news story about what happened, to something serious but far less apocalyptic. I am not saying there is no potential for escalation, but in the months after September 11, the reality of anthrax looked more like the paragraph above and less like the popular scenarios.

In addition to sinister use of biological pathogens, chemical attacks have also actually happened, and the outcomes of those undertakings were also far different from what we'd been led to expect. Here's what happened in the most famous case: A Japanese sect called Aum Shinrikyo undertook a chemical attack in the Tokyo subway system — an ideal environment for maximum fatalities because it is enclosed, has limited ventilation, and has tens of thousands of people unable to get away easily. Still, even with nearly perfect conditions for the attack, less than 10 percent of the people in the subway were injured, all but a few of those who experienced any effects were better within a few hours, and only 1 percent of those injured died. Were the perpetrators just incompetent? Hardly; the group's membership included highly trained bioscientists and chemists. Were they underfunded? Hardly; they had millions of dollars to spend. Were they rushed? Not at all; they had lots of time for research and preparation. Did they fail? Utterly.

In what way did they fail? Well, first of all, they failed to harm and kill lots of people. Second, they failed to shut down the Japanese government. And mostly, they failed to make reality match imagination, and that's going to happen a lot.

To be clear, my point here is not that bad things don't happen — I am deeply involved in managing bad things that happen all the time. My point is not that there's nothing to worry about — there's plenty you can worry about. Rather, my point is that the popular worst-case scenarios are just that: popular — and they remain so as long as they offer drama and, perhaps surprisingly, as long as they don't happen. Once a terrible thing happens, it moves from our imaginations to our reality; it moves from being an interesting possible problem to something about which we must choose real and immediate solutions. We respond. We manage, even when faced with tidal waves and nature's stunning time bombs: volcanic eruptions and earthquakes. These are clear and powerful dangers; of course, though understandably, we are more afraid of the danger that is conscious, the danger that emerges from the malicious intent we face today.

So let's explore some of the malicious possibilities that occupy our attention so that we can place them into the appropriate mental compartments. Once compartmentalized, the information will be available if needed and will not blind us to the rest of life when not needed. As opposed to inviting these outcomes to be houseguests, we'll look at them from a distance: because that's where they actually are — at a distance.

■　■　■

Chemical weapons are toxic substances, normally in gas or liquid form, that someone seeks to get onto or into human beings. They act immediately on physiological systems to cause debilitation or death.

Biological weapons are bacteria and viruses that are intentionally introduced into human hosts. (This was previously called "germ warfare.") Once inside, they propagate and cause disease. There is always a period of time, called an incubation period, between the time of first exposure and when disease symptoms appear.

These hazards together can be abbreviated as "biochem."

In recent times you have no doubt gained an unusual education about biochem agents by assembling fragments of information from reporters, scientists, and talking heads whose expertise ranges from dubious to impressive. While I do not intend what follows to be a comprehensive treatise about biochem weapons, I do want to provide an accurate foundation onto which you can continue to add new information. To help, I sought out two experts who might seem like polar opposites: an internationally known scientist and a retired soldier.

Dr. Raymond Zilinskas is a consultant to my firm on biochem issues, selected because of his impeccable credentials as a United Nations weapons inspector and senior scientist at the Center for Nonproliferation Research at the Monterey Institute of International Studies.

Sergeant First Class Red Thomas is a retired weapons, munitions, and training expert from the U.S. Army. Since he was seven years old, Red has had, as he puts it, "a penchant for learning about anything that goes bang, boom, or pop."

Dr. Zilinskas, tired of seeing so much misinformation on the TV news, offers sober thinking, keen intellect, and exceptional communication skills to help his country understand the actual risks during these times. Red Thomas explains his contribution more simply: "I was watching these ninnies on the news, and I hurt for all the people I knew were afraid."

Though Dr. Zilinskas is in the business of considering worst-case scenarios, he points out that "these are worrisome times, but let us not overestimate the hazard. For the average American citizen, the probability of being affected by a bioterrorist attack is *vanishingly low.*" Neither Dr. Zilinskas nor Red Thomas believes we will see the kinds of devastating attacks often portrayed in TV news stories, in which tens of thousands of people are harmed or killed.

CHEMICAL ATTACKS

Red Thomas recalls a *60 Minutes* segment in which someone reported that one drop of nerve gas could kill a thousand people: "Well, he didn't tell you the thousand dead people per drop was theoretical. Drill sergeants exaggerate how terrible this stuff is to keep the recruits awake in class. I know this because I was a drill sergeant, too. *Forget everything you've ever seen on TV, in the movies, or read in a novel about this stuff; it was all a lie.*"

Though media reports and politicians characterize chemical agents as "weapons of mass destruction," this appears to be the wrong category. The only weapons of mass destruction on earth are bombs (with nuclear bombs being the most dangerous). Red Thomas points out that chemical weapons are not made for mass destruction — they are made for "area denial" and terror. As he says, "When you leave the area, you almost always leave the risk. That's the difference between you and a soldier: You can leave the area and the risk; soldiers may have to stay put and sit through it, and that's why they need all that spiffy gear."

Dr. Zilinskas has made clear that many difficulties would have to be overcome before someone could inflict mass casualties with chemicals. Adds Red: "This stuff won't work when it's freezing, it doesn't last when it's hot, and wind spreads it too thin too fast. They've got to get this stuff on you, or get you to inhale it, for it to work. They also have to get the concentration of chemicals high enough to kill or wound someone. Too little and it's nothing, too much and it's wasted. A chemical-weapons attack that kills a lot of people is incredibly hard to do even with military-grade agents and equipment."

Although nerve agents may sound like science fiction, Red brings the truth home:

> You have nerve agents in your house; plain old bug killer (like Raid) is a nerve agent. All nerve agents work the same way: They are cholinesterase inhibitors that mess up the signals your nervous system uses to make your body function. It can harm you if you get it on your skin, but it works best if they can get you to inhale it. If a person doesn't die in the first minute and can leave the area, he's probably going to live.

The military's treatment response for all nerve agents is atropine and pralidoxime chloride [usually called 2-pam chloride]. Neither one of these does anything to cure the nerve agent; what they do is send the body into overdrive to keep a person alive for five minutes — after that the agent is used up. The best protection is fresh air and staying calm.

The symptoms for nerve-agent contamination include everything you'd imagine: sudden headache, dimmed vision, runny nose, excessive saliva or drooling, difficulty breathing, tightness in chest, nausea, stomach cramps. (There can also be an odor of hay, green corn, something fruity, or camphor.) In the unlikely event you ever experience these symptoms in public, Red Thomas suggests you ask yourself, "Did anything out of the ordinary just happen? A loud pop? Did someone spray something on the crowd? Are other people getting sick, too?"

Again, it's highly unlikely, but if the answer to these questions is yes, then remaining calm is key, because panic leads to faster breathing and, accordingly, more inhalation of poison. Next, leave the area immediately; get outside. Fresh air is your best immediate treatment, what Red Thomas calls the "right-now antidote." If some thick liquid is actually on you, your natural inclination is the wisest: Get it off you, blotting or scraping it off with something disposable — and get away from it.

If you get away and lessen your exposure, the risk drops. Red Thomas moves this fear from the paralyzing to the practical: "Remember, people trying to hurt you with nerve agents have to do all the work; they have to get the concentration up and keep it up for several minutes. All you have to do is quit getting it on you and quit breathing it by putting space between you and the attack."

Another category of chemical weapons is called blood agents (cyanide or arsine that affect the blood's ability to provide oxygen). The scenario for attack using these poisons would likely be the same as for nerve agents. The symptoms include blue lips, blue under the fingernails, rapid breathing. The military's recommended treatment is amyl nitrite. As with nerve agents, the treatment is just to keep your body working for five minutes till the toxins are used up. As with nerve agents, immediate fresh air is important.

BIOLOGICAL ATTACKS

Bacillus anthracis, which causes anthrax, currently the biological pathogen causing the greatest concern, cannot be spread in many ways. The anthrax spore is dormant and dry. Merely touching it does not give you anthrax. If you have a cut on your finger, and you touch anthrax spores, you might come down with the skin form of anthrax — or you might not. The same is true of the two other kinds of anthrax infection: in the digestive tract, usually gotten from eating infected meat or otherwise ingesting many spores, or in the lungs, which victims get from deeply inhaling anthrax spores that become airborne. Whatever type, anthrax is not contagious person to person — and many people who are exposed don't ever develop the disease.

Dr. Zilinskas advises that terrorists trying to harm lots of people with airborne pathogens are likely to have relatively little success because of the technical difficulty in formulating pathogens and toxins for wide-range airborne dispersal. It would be difficult to develop and operate dispersal mechanisms successfully, and difficult to ensure proper meteorological conditions for effective dispersal. Air temperature, ground temperature, humidity, sunlight, precipitation, wind speed, and obstacles such as buildings and terrain all influence the success of any effort to disperse biochem agents.

Adds Red Thomas: "Saddam Hussein spent twenty years and millions of dollars, and he couldn't get it right — so you can imagine how hard it would be for terrorists. The more you know about this stuff, the more you realize how hard it is to use."

Even without directly affecting large numbers of people, anthrax and other biological agents cause great fear, leading observers to forget that naturally occurring infectious diseases are far more dangerous — as proved throughout human history. Says Dr. Zilinskas: "In comparison to the real and enormous hazard of naturally occurring infectious diseases, the problem of deliberately caused disease is almost insignificant." In other words, while we worry about a handful of people who are intent on doing something destructive with biological pathogens, literally billions of bacteria are working to get into your body and cause trouble. During the period in which one person died each week from anthrax, recognize that about four hundred times as many people died from flu-related ailments, and few of us bother to even get a flu shot.

You may also have been concerned about terrorist attacks where food is contaminated, and indeed, such attacks have occurred. Dr. Zilinskas notes: "Much like what has taken place in the past, these attacks are likely to harm people ranging in number from a few to hundreds — not thousands." (As mentioned in chapter 1, ten restaurant salad bars and one supermarket were contaminated by members of the Rajneeshee cult in Oregon in 1984. There were 751 people affected. All recovered fully.)

You have likely also heard worst-case scenarios about bubonic and pneumonic plague. Bubonic plague is not communicable from human to human; pneumonic plague is communicable, but all plague can be treated with commonly available antibiotics. You may also have heard speculation about botulinum toxin; it is deadly if untreated, but it can be treated with an antitoxin.

And finally, there's smallpox, which is caused by a terrible virus that was declared eradicated worldwide in 1980. Though anything is possible, the smallpox virus officially exists in just two places on earth: at a U.S. research facility and at a Russian research facility. There is an effective vaccine for smallpox, and the U.S. government has millions of doses and millions more are currently being produced.

Dr. Zilinskas and I agree that smallpox is an unattractive biological weapon for a terrorist organization with political goals, particularly if the organization is state-sponsored (and governments are the most likely institutions to be able to get the smallpox virus). The reason a government is likely to continue discouraging the terroristic use of small-pox: The more successfully the virus is spread, the more likely the same virus will make its way back to the sponsoring country. In other words, were Iraq to sponsor spreading smallpox (as unlikely and difficult as that may be), if many people in a target country were infected, it becomes a near certainty that people in Iraq would become infected as well. No nation on earth would be better able to deal with the public-health emergency than the United States — so to the precise degree that a perpetrator succeeds, the sponsoring nation loses.

Accordingly, unless an individual or group has apocalyptic visions (the destruction of everything and everyone — and Middle Eastern terrorists have not been apocalyptic), spreading highly infectious diseases is counterproductive to virtually every political aim one could imagine.

Though it's clear we shall always be vulnerable to bio-chem weapons (as we are vulnerable to naturally occurring viruses and bacteria), several important steps have been taken in the past few years. For example, the U.S. armed forces have organized and trained rapid-response teams to survey attack sites and initiate decontamination procedures. Many state and local agencies have received federal funding for equipment and training and have participated in exercises that help anticipate and prepare for meeting our needs in a biochem emergency. That's why hundreds of agencies have the protective clothing, other specialized equipment, and training you saw as they responded to suspicious powders and hoaxes all over America. I don't mean to say that every possibility has been fully anticipated or prepared for, because that's not the case. However, during the weeks following 9/11 useful new knowledge about anthrax was evolving right before our eyes. You probably already know a lot about treatment plans and symptoms, and more information is available to you as it develops. (See Appendix A.)

Also, consider that our government agencies have lots of experience in responding to incidents of accidental chemical and biological contamination. Reassuringly, the response to a chemical gas attack would not be unlike the procedures currently used for responding to an overturned railroad tank car full of contaminants. Several outbreaks of Legionnaire's disease (a biological hazard) have been successfully handled by authorities around the nation.

Dr. Zilinskas advises that when an outbreak of disease is first detected, officials are not immediately in a position to know whether the outbreak was intentional or natural. Thus, the initial public health and medical response to a disease outbreak is the same, whatever its origin.

If government officials detect a chemical or biological attack, they will likely issue specific civil-defense warnings through the media. In most cases — unless you happen to be at the actual site of the chemical or biological agents — you are likely to have time to take the one precaution that applies to all biochem hazards: avoiding areas near the contamination.

NONMILITARY NUCLEAR ATTACK

A nuclear device used by terrorists would be low-yield; it would not, contrary to our worst imaginings, level whole cities. Effects would likely be limited to a half-mile circle (not that much different from the area of damage at the World Trade Center). But when it's done, it's done. People within the affected area who live through the heat, blast, and initial burst of radiation are likely to continue living for as long as they would have in any event. As Red Thomas says, "Radiation will not create fifty-foot-tall women, giant ants, or grasshoppers the size of tanks."

There are many kinds of radiation, but three are most relevant to our topic: alpha, beta, and gamma. The others you have lived with for years. Red Thomas explains: "You need to worry about what is called ionizing radiation. It's the same as people getting radiation treatments for cancer, only a bigger area gets radiated. The good news is you don't have to just sit there and take it, and there's lots you can do rather than panic. First, your skin will stop alpha particles and a page of a newspaper or your clothing will stop beta particles; you've just got to try to avoid inhaling dust that's contaminated with atoms that are emitting these things and you'll be generally safe." Gamma rays are the most dangerous, but it also takes a lot of them to kill people.

Overall preparation for any terrorist attack that would result in major damage is the same as one would wisely take for a big storm or earthquake. How has Red Thomas prepared?

If you want a gas mask, fine, go get one. I know this stuff and I'm not getting one, and I told my mom not to bother with one, either. How's that for confidence? We have a week's worth of cash, several days' worth of canned goods, and plenty of soap and water.

These terrorists can't conceive of a nation this big with this many resources. Biochem and small nuclear weapons are made to cause panic and terror and to demoralize. The government is going nuts over this stuff because they have to protect every inch of America. You've only got to protect yourself, and by doing that, you help the country.

CREDIBLE THREATS, WARNING SIGNS, AND KANGAROOS

Since we are the editors of which scenarios get in and which are invested with credibility, it's important to evaluate our sources of information. I explained this during a presentation to hundreds of government threat assessors at the Central Intelligence Agency a few years ago, making my point by drawing on a very rare safety hazard: kangaroo attacks. I told the audience that about twenty people a year are killed by the normally friendly animals and that kangaroos always display a specific set of indicators before they attack:

1. They give what appears to be a wide and genial smile (but they are actually baring their teeth).
2. They check their pouches compulsively several times to be sure they have no young with them (they never attack while carrying young).

3. They look behind them (since they always retreat immediately after they kill).

After these three signals, they lunge, brutally pummel their victim, and then gallop off.

I asked two audience members to stand up and repeat back the warning signs, and both flawlessly described the smile, the checking of the pouch for young, and the looking back for an escape route. In fact, everyone in that room (and now you) will remember those warning signs for life. Your brain is wired to value such information, and if you are ever face-to-face with a kangaroo, be it tomorrow or decades from now, those three pre-incident indicators will be in your head.

The problem, I told the audience at the CIA, is that I made up those signals. I did it to demonstrate the risk of inaccurate information. I actually know nothing about kangaroo behavior (so forget the three signals if you can — or stay away from hostile kangaroos).

In our lives, we are constantly bombarded with kangaroo facts masquerading as knowledge, but what we will give credence to is up to us.

For example, in the months following 9/11, we were often warned about new major acts of terrorism predicted to occur within days. Government officials and newsreaders spoke of "credible threats," a phrase often confused with high likelihood, but let's break it down: A threat is a statement of an intention to do harm, period. Credible means plausible, and it can sometimes mean believable. In the context of the world since 9/11, any threat spoken by extremists is believable.

Politicians and newsreaders often use the word *threat* as if it is interchangeable with *hazard*. Threats and hazards are two different things. *Hazard* means a chance of being injured or harmed. (The root of the word actually comes from a dice game.) A threat is something someone expresses. Accordingly, when the U.S. attorney general speaks of a credible threat, if he is using his terms correctly, he is telling us about something someone has expressed.

Threats are generally spoken specifically to cause fear and anxiety. That's not my intent right now, so please pardon my saying this: I am going to kill you.

There, you have just received a death threat. I am a credible person who is capable and well versed in the ways of violence, so it's a credible threat, too. This threat you just received is vastly more direct, clear, demonstrable, and well documented than most of the terrorist threats you've heard about.

Press conferences that warn of terrorist strikes "within the next two days" understandably cause lots of uncertainty. For example, the governor of California announced a "credible threat" against landmark bridges in California and warned that the attacks would take place between November 1 and November 9. Upon what in the world do they base these schedules? Is the underlying premise that some terrorist said, "If I haven't done this by the ninth, I'll get over it, and I wouldn't dream of doing it on, say, the fourteenth. So your risk is just between the first and the ninth."

In any event, after the governor's "credible threat" had caused concern to Californians for a few days, the FBI described it as "not credible." Incredible, isn't it?

A lot of the warnings we've received from public officials might as well be threats themselves, for they have the same effect. The row of serious men behind the podium and the choice of alarming words often obscure underlying information that is pretty thin. The drama of these presentations is tantamount to having your doctor call you in, sit you down, and put one hand on your shoulder as he thumbs through your charts with the other. He levels a serious look at you, and just before you pass out, he says: "Your test results are in, and in my opinion, you're going to be fine."

I am certain that most officials who announce threats mean well, but it sometimes seems that everybody wants to be Rudy Giuliani. Since only Rudy really is, others could help us more if they advised the public along these lines: "You may notice extra National Guardsmen at various bridges. This is a precaution in response to some threats and speculation we have assessed. As you've seen in recent weeks, no threats have been successfully acted upon, and we'll do our part to ensure that these threats remain in that category. We'll take special care protecting the bridges, and if you see anything that concerns you, please make a report."

Ideally, a press conference about threats to the Golden Gate Bridge would be held on the Golden Gate Bridge.

Alarming words — whether spoken by some angry extremist or by our own public officials — cause people to react by going into a defensive posture, psychologically speaking. Though the words themselves can't put us at any actual risk, uncertainty about risk causes alarm, which causes a problem: When we are stunned or distracted, we raise the very drawbridge — perception — that we must cross in order to make successful predictions.

In the past thirty years, I've read, heard, and seen the world's most creative, gruesome, distasteful, effective, and well-performed threats. I've learned that it's important to react calmly, because when in alarm we stop evaluating information mindfully and start doing it physically.

For example, a death threat communicated in a letter or phone call cannot possibly pose any immediate hazard, but the recipient might nonetheless start getting physically ready for danger with the increased breathing and heart-beat to support all the fear-response chemicals and systems. These responses are valuable when facing present danger, but for assessing future hazard, staying calm produces better results. A way to do this is to consciously ask and answer the question "Am I in immediate danger?" Your body wants you to get this question out of the way, and once you do, you'll be free to keep perceiving what's going on.

Though thoughts of harming you may be terrible, they are also inevitable. Many people around the world (and even in America) hate America, some enough to actually harm us, others enough to want to harm us, many enough to threaten harm, and many others enough to be glad when we are harmed. Until 9/11 most people in the world had never seen Americans as human, vulnerable, or part of the world community. Our aloofness and our success bred envy. It is particularly difficult for Americans to fully believe and accept that people hate us so fiercely, and there has been lots of denial about this truth. Individual Americans can feel that they are just going about their lives, but that in itself — without your doing another thing — has been fuel for aggression. It's understandable that this aggression causes so much fear because it seems to many as if it came out of nowhere. It didn't, but whatever the reasons, all these thoughts about harming us are themselves harming us.

Thoughts are not the problem, of course; the expression of thought is what causes us anxiety, and most of the time that's the whole idea. Understanding this will help reduce unwarranted fear.

That someone would intrude on our peace of mind, that they would speak words so difficult to take back, that they would exploit our fear of flying, that they would care so little about us, that they would raise the stakes so high, that they would stoop so low — all of this alarms us, and by design.

Threatening words are dispatched like soldiers under strict orders: Cause anxiety that cannot be ignored. Surprisingly, their deployment isn't entirely bad news. It's bad, of course, that someone threatens violence, but the threat means that at least for now the speaker has considered violence and decided against it. The threat means that at least for now the speaker favors words that alarm over actions that harm.

For an instrument of communication used so frequently, the threat is little understood, until you think about it. The parent who threatens punishment, the lawyer who threatens unspecified "further action," the head of state who threatens war, the terrorist group that threatens mass killing, the child who threatens to make a scene — all are using words with the exact same intent: to cause uncertainty.

Though you wouldn't know it by the reaction they frequently earn, threats are rarely spoken from a position of power. Whatever power threats have is derived from the fear instilled in the victim, for fear is the currency of the threatener. How one responds to a threat determines whether it will be a valuable instrument or mere words. Thus, it is the listener and not the speaker — we and not the terrorists — who decides how powerful a threat will be.

In most instances of terrorist threat, the threat is the terrorist event. It is the end in itself. Speaking generally, those who threaten do not act, and those who act do not threaten.

What often happens, however, is that a threat refers to a previous terrorist act, thus attaching to the current threat the potency of the past tragedy. For example, after the bombing of the Oklahoma City federal building, any threat about blowing up a federal building conjured the original act and caused great anxiety. Hundreds of federal buildings were modified in response to an incident that happens, in effect, once every 230 years. Nobody would want Timothy McVeigh to be among this nation's most influential architects, but that's one of the results of over-reaction.

A shooting from the sidewalk and we add bulletproof

windows. Then a bomb in the lobby and we add X-ray machines and explosives-sniffing dogs. Then a bomb *outside* the building and we add vehicle barricades. Then a shooting from across the highway — as happened to CIA employees as they arrived at work one morning — and what do we do, add a fence around all the buildings? Some precautions aren't reducing risk so much as moving it around.

The point to remember when we think about what terrorists might do next is this: By its very nature, terrorism surprises us. It's true that there are sometimes trends in which several people or groups mimic a particular kind of act, but the overall history of terrorism is that it changes. Terrorists try to do unpredictable things. The terrorist's imagination begins where the security expert's imagination (and budget) ends. Precautions that are reactionary, such as concrete barriers around *every* federal building (as opposed to those that are clearly special targets), end up costing us a lot, without making much difference to terrorism.

Our social world relies on our investing some threats with credibility while discounting others. Our belief that they really will tow the car if we leave it here encourages us to look for a parking space unencumbered by that particular threat. The disbelief that our joking spouse will really kill us if we are late to dinner allows us to stay in the marriage. And finally, we are better able to go about our day-to-day lives with the knowledge that most of the time, terrorists with the power to act, act, and those without the power to act threaten.

■ ■ ■

Something often missing from worst-case scenarios is consideration of best-case management and response. Although it is difficult to fully prepare for every kind of emergency, it's clear that the U.S. government has extraordinary disaster-response capability. Throughout your life, you have seen our government respond with remarkable effectiveness to unusual and unpredictable occurrences (earthquakes, floods, hurricanes, fires, bombings, workplace-violence incidents, outbreaks of disease, and even attacks with jetliners). Those of us present during the Los Angeles earthquake, a devastating natural disaster, recall the rapid resumption of all utilities, the effectiveness of law enforcement, and a faster return to normal life than other nations facing the same challenges could likely imagine. The resources of our federal government, and those of state and local agencies, far outdistance any in world history. If we have learned anything from the emergencies we have experienced in our lives, it is that our infrastructure is strong, resilient, and capable.

For example, following the attacks on the World Trade Center, New York City, the state of New York, and the federal government brought together resources far beyond what most scenarios would have included. When I toured ground zero at the World Trade Center days after the attack, I was impressed to see emergency responders from all over the nation. I saw police officers from Sacramento, firefighters from Miami, medical officials from Detroit, and police cars and ambulances from other faraway cities. I saw personnel from every government agency one can think of. I even saw firefighters from Canada. Public and private resources worked together in astonishing ways, including the preparation of *thirty thousand* meals a day served around the clock to emergency workers (under the heroic direction of a restaurateur named David Boulet, who, along with an army of dedicated volunteers, made it his mission in life to feed emergency workers).

Having been closely involved in many emergencies and crises throughout my career, it reassures me to see the flexibility and industriousness of Americans (both in and out of government), particularly when things occur that we either could not or did not precisely predict. In fact, I find our ability to respond to the unpredicted calamities to be far more impressive than our ability to plan for the predictable ones. Prediction itself is an uncertain science, of course, but the ability of our government and our people to respond is quite certain. Remember, when any country on earth experiences some gigantic disaster, it is the United States that is most often looked to for help — because we're the country in the best position to provide it.

■　■　■

We all feel some uncertainty these days, and indeed these are uncertain times — like all times. Even so, there are things about which we can be certain: We can be certain that life doesn't give us anything we can't handle — and that's been proved by our management of every challenge we have faced together as a nation. And we can be certain that terrorist threats are not guarantees of action and, in fact, *are usually in place of action.* These certainties allow us to go about our daily lives; you remember, the daily lives that derive so much of their variety and vitality from uncertainty.

7

SAFER THAN DRIVING
TO THE AIRPORT — STILL

September 30, 2001

As I write this, I am sitting on a United Airlines flight from Los Angeles bound for New York City. Looking toward the cockpit of this 767 is like being on the set of a play I've seen a hundred times, for that's how often I've imagined this view since September 11. That's how many times I've played over in my head the experience of the crew and passengers — and the hijackers — on those four flights. I obsessed over the tiny details, not to be morbid but rather to be enlightened, to learn whatever I could from bringing my knowledge of violence and predatory crime to this precise space and situation.

I am imagining the opportunity Atta must have waited for: the fastest and easiest way into the cockpit. Just as I am doing now, and from the same vantage point, he watched the flight attendants. He knew that soon after takeoff, one of them would enter the cockpit to see if the pilots wanted some coffee or a snack. Atta knew that after a minute or so, the door would open again. Then, he and his comrades could easily push the flight attendant aside and enter the cockpit. They would find the stunned pilots strapped in their seats, absolutely unready and unable to defend themselves. The pilots would have every reason to expect some exchange of words with the intruders, to be ordered to fly somewhere, and the pilots would have been willing to comply. But instead, the pilots would be brutally and wordlessly attacked until fully incapacitated, and then pulled from their seats.

In the main cabin, another of Atta's men would be holding up a device he claimed was a bomb. He would bark instructions, then threats, then promises that everything would be all right, then threats again. As the passengers moved into seats at the back of the plane, they would do all they could to avoid upsetting the hijackers. Soon, they would hear a heavily accented but reassuring announcement over the loudspeaker: "Stay in your seats. We are returning to the airport." Like the pilots before them, the passengers would have every reason to assume they would be all right if they just cooperated — except for the passengers on Flight 93, who knew better.

In spite of the grimness of the subject, the exploration into airline security begun on that United flight has left me feeling far more hopeful than when I started. I found that passengers today are safer from hijacking than they've been at any time in the past. Right now, today, it is safer to take a commercial flight than it is to take a shower, safer to fly across the country than to drive to work, safer to ride on an American Airlines jumbo jet than to ride on a Greyhound bus. Even today.

Yet many travelers remain unconvinced about airline security, and I believe that's because it is unconvincing. We just feel it, we just know that confiscating nail clippers is not the answer. We just know that having lots of armed men around the passenger-screening point brilliantly protects the X-ray machines but does not address the core of the issue. We see air security debated by politicians, regulatory agencies, the airlines, and lobbyists for pilots, mechanics, flight attendants, air-traffic controllers. The only people who aren't represented are the passengers, and yet it is the passengers who actually make air travel safe. Most of the issues you've been told matter so much really don't matter so much — and I know that may be hard to imagine, but I believe you'll find in the coming pages that it's so.

Some of what you're about to read may at first seem discouraging, but please stay with me. The destination in sight — if we do just a few easy things — is that we shall all have far more peace of mind about commercial air travel. That in turn will help others resume flying, which will help the major airlines, and that will help us all. In this chapter, I'm writing mostly about anti-hijacking strategies, but also about the ways America responds to security challenges, and also about you and me — and the comfort we can justifiably feel when flying commercially.

■　■　■

Though there are thousands of security precautions, they all fit into two broad categories:

Category One: Those implemented to reduce risk
Category Two: Those implemented to reduce
    anxiety

Both types of precaution are important and both have meaning, but they are not the same. Unfortunately, when it comes to security, the American way has often been to implement procedures that are more relevant to assuaging public anxiety than they are to reducing risk. After the shootings at Columbine, officials around the nation publicized that cameras had been installed in high schools — a perfect example of a Category Two security response (designed more to reduce anxiety than risk), particularly since Columbine had plenty of cameras, cameras that could do nothing to prevent the shootings. Were this a longer book, I could share dozens of times that Category Two security precautions were implemented and announced, dozens of times that the responses to fear-provoking incidents were more about getting us to shut up and stop worrying than about really addressing risk.

There's one particularly instructive example right now: After 9/11, buses had become the comforting alternative to flying for thousands of jittery travelers — a resurrection of sorts for the Greyhound company. But it didn't last long.

About three weeks after the 9/11 attacks, a Croatian national named Damir Igric was a passenger on a Greyhound bus traveling from Chicago to Orlando. He made two trips to the front of the bus to ask people to trade seats with him. Both refused. Soon after, Igric walked to the front of the bus for the third time and, without hesitation, slashed the driver's throat with a box cutter, pulled the driver out of the seat, and steered the bus off the highway. Igric and six others died, and thirty were injured.

Within two weeks, another Greyhound passenger ran to the front of the bus and attacked the driver. This time, passengers quickly intervened and subdued the man, and nobody was hurt.

Just one day later, still another Greyhound passenger attacked a driver. Again, passengers solved the problem immediately, grappling with the man so the driver could stop the bus safely. This attacker reportedly ranted about hijacking and threatened to flip the bus, but a Greyhound spokesperson mindful of troubling publicity suggested that the man be characterized as "an unruly passenger" and not a hijacker.

Within days of this frightening incident, a powerful military explosive called C-4 was found in a public storage locker at a Greyhound bus station in Philadelphia.

So, over the span of just a few days, beleaguered executives at Greyhound found themselves facing a major loss of public confidence, and something had to be done.

What was the main security procedure they implemented and announced to curtail hijacking and attacks on their drivers? "Passengers will no longer be allowed to sit in the seats immediately behind the driver."

Prohibiting use of the front seats does not improve security for bus passengers in any way at all. I feel sympathy for the Greyhound company, which had an awful time in 2001 (there'd also been two serious accidents just before September in which many were injured and two were killed). But their proposal to keep the front seats empty is a classic Category Two security procedure. Even a cursory look at the cases reminds us that none of the first three men who attacked Greyhound drivers after 9/11 had been sitting in the front seats anyway, and far more important, some of the passengers who saved the second and third buses were able to do so precisely because they *were* sitting in those seats!

Within two weeks of implementing the restriction about the front seats, still another Greyhound passenger attacked the driver. This time, there was nobody near enough to intervene, and the attacker successfully caused the bus to flip over, injuring thirty people.

Why did Greyhound implement a nonsense security procedure that actually increased risk? Because the kind of Category Two response they announced usually works in America, by which I mean that the public seems to say, "Oh, uh-huh, they've taken steps, looks good," and then goes back to sleep.

Let's not do that with airline security.

It may seem unlikely that an issue the government and the people care about so much wouldn't be resolved effectively, but take a look at this passage from a *New York Times* article:

> The head of the Federal Aviation Administration announced today that his agency would soon propose a rule requiring airlines to place a bulletproof shield around pilots to protect them. . . . Until now, the airlines in this country have followed the wishes of hijackers to provide maximum assurances that no one would be hurt.

The article goes on to say that Tuesday's incident "seemed to put a new face on the problem."

Yes, Tuesday's incident being a suicide mission did indeed put a new face on the problem, but the article wasn't about Tuesday, September 11. It was a Tuesday way back in 1970, one that also stunned the nation's air travelers.

An Eastern Airlines passenger named John Devivo told a flight attendant that he wanted to speak with the captain. Passengers saw the flight attendant walk the man up the aisle and admit him to the cockpit — though they didn't see why she did it.

Inside, Captain Robert Wilbur and co-pilot James Hartley were busy on final approach to Logan Airport. They turned and got the answer: The man was aiming a gun at them. Captain Wilbur advised the flight attendant, "It's okay, go tell the passengers everything is all right." Devivo ordered the pilots to head the jetliner out to sea and "just fly till the plane runs out of gas." When the pilots hesitated, the gunman fired one shot into co-pilot Hartley. Though wounded, Hartley wrestled the gun away and used it to shoot Devivo twice. Several shots had been fired by this point, at least one bullet even passing through the cockpit door back into the passenger cabin.

The jet dipped a bit, but Captain Wilbur regained control. He looked over to see Devivo slumped on the floor, and Captain Hartley slumped in his seat. Compartmentalizing the terrible realization that Hartley was dying next to him, Wilbur continued to fly the jet. As he operated the controls, he came to another terrible realization: He himself was shot in both arms. Still another terrible realization: The assailant was regaining consciousness and coming toward him again. Wilbur used the gun to strike the assailant back down, and quickly landed the plane.

This incident of tragedy and heroism spawned media reports, questions about aviation security, and occurrences like many we saw after 9/11. For example, one man was taken off a plane after a flight attendant overheard him saying how easy it would be to kill a pilot. On questioning him, police learned that the man was a member of Congress. He acknowledged how "understandably uptight people are and the feeling of helplessness they have."

In short, we've been here before, but in 1970, FAA officials had never seen a suicidal hijacking, and maybe that's why they didn't follow through on their own proposal to make cockpits entry-resistant. Actually that was the *second* time the recommendation was proposed and then left unimplemented. Let's not have a third.

Actually, we can't have a third, because we had it in 1974 when a man named Samuel Byck, armed with a handgun and a gasoline bomb, shot his way onto a Delta Airlines jet at the Baltimore airport, intending to crash the plane into the White House (sound familiar?). He killed a security guard and shot the pilot and co-pilot before police shot him.

We can't have a fourth, either, because in 1986, a passenger named David Burke stormed into the cockpit of a jetliner over San Diego and shot both pilots. He crashed the plane into the ground, and all forty-three on board died.

And we can't have a fifth, because in 1994, a Federal Express employee named Auburn Calloway attacked the pilots with two hammers. Though sustaining several serious injuries, the co-pilot and flight engineer were able to get Calloway out of the cockpit, allowing the pilot to land the plane. Calloway's plan had been to kill the pilots and crash the plane.

We can't have a sixth, either, because later in 1994, in a plan strikingly similar to 9/11, members of a fanatical terror squad known as the Armed Islamic Group took over an Air France jetliner. Their plan was to fly it into the Eiffel Tower in Paris and detonate explosives on board just before impact. The hijackers were killed by French commandos who stormed the plane when it was on the ground for refueling.

Having ignored the lessons of all these suicide hijackings, the FAA and the rest of us witnessed a seventh, eighth, ninth, and tenth — all on the same day.

The process of preventing hijacking requires, in my opinion, a small adjustment in thinking because even the name most people use to define the issue — airport security — is part of the problem. Forget for a moment about airport security, and think about *airline* security. To some this may seem no distinction at all, but it is the critical distinction.

Although many precautions have relevance to our safety

when flying, all the cases you just read about, including the four you saw with your own eyes, make clear that the mission in front of us can be stated in three sentences:

> The key precaution in airline security is in the air, not on the ground. It is an effective entry-resistant cockpit door that is religiously kept closed throughout every flight. The passengers and cabin crews will do the rest.

I suggest that for a moment we set aside talk of weapons screening, baggage searches, profiling, ID cards, watch lists, fences, tarmac access, doubling the training and salaries of screeners, and making them federal employees. I suggest we do something very rare amidst the cacophony of special-interest propaganda: *Focus on one thing at a time.* Let's fully explore the most serious, resolvable problems in airline security — and resolve them. Above all, let's be certain we don't accept any security proposals from Category Two when Category One precautions are actually less expensive and more effective.

KEEP THE COCKPIT DOORS CLOSED AND LOCKED

I have flown both United Airlines and American Airlines since 9/11, and based on that admittedly limited sample, I found American Airlines personnel to be far more watchful about protecting the cockpit. (I'm not assuming what I saw on United is the norm, but it is what I saw.) On that United Airlines flight soon after 9/11, I wrote:

When I boarded, I was disappointed to see the cockpit door open as the passengers walked to their seats, but since we've lifted off, those of us who can see the cockpit door are comforted that it's closed and locked.

But the comfort does not last long. Just this moment the cockpit door was opened wide as a tray of food was carried in. The door is left open while the flight attendant got some other item from the galley. This is occurring while one male passenger is standing in the area waiting for another male passenger to leave the bathroom. In other words, two men are immediately in the vicinity of the open cockpit. Strengthening of cockpit doors has been discussed in every newspaper and on every news show in the country. If it's worthwhile to improve the locks, isn't it worthwhile to use them, and to keep the doors closed and locked whenever possible?

At least during these times with so many terrorist warnings, could not each pilot bring along a tuna sandwich, an apple, some cookies, and a thermos of coffee for the five-hour flight to New York — and keep the door closed?

Are we really serious about aviation security? We never have been before, and if even pilots and flight attendants are not worried enough to keep that door shut, the public probably won't retain its will to stay serious about this. The flight attendant just opened the cockpit door again and is now standing in the open doorway, having a jokey exchange with the pilots. Another flight attendant just joined in, both now standing in the open doorway with their backs to the passengers.

Taxicabs in New York City provide more entry resistance and bullet resistance for drivers than jetliners provide for pilots. And a New York taxi driver carrying two male passengers late at night wouldn't open up the bullet-resistant divider every few miles. Subway operators in most cities also have better protection than do airline pilots — even today, even after improvements to the cockpit doors.

One of the things that currently happens on flights is that after a while, flight attendants become familiar and comfortable with passengers, and their guard goes way down. They are in a service business; they are not suspicious police detectives. What flight attendants and pilots alike are remarkably professional at is following regulations — and that's what they need from government right now. From the airlines' point of view, since keeping the cockpit doors closed and locked is a procedural change and not a structural change, it has no financial cost whatsoever — and limitless potential for benefit.

PASSENGER SCREENING

One could make the argument that since passengers are screened more carefully since 9/11, crew members have less to be concerned about. It may be natural to want to shift the responsibility to a screener at an airport you left behind a thousand miles ago, but the responsibility for air security is right where you are: in the air.

Passenger screening will always have limited effectiveness. It is, at best, a deterrent to some people who might otherwise carry a firearm on board. But with a billion screenings every year, there are going to be failures. One recent federal report found that seven out of twenty airport-security employees failed basic competency tests. As you read on, you may wonder about the basic competence of some senior government officials as well — but it's easier to blame the hourly employees at the airport, I suppose.

If flight attendants and pilots take any comfort because of America's success at confiscating nail clippers from passengers, they have plenty of reasons to think again. For example, on October 23, 2001, during the so-called high alert at airports, a man carried a loaded gun onto a commercial flight at the New Orleans airport — by accident.

The incident pointed out again that the system isn't perfect, but the solution chosen was more discouraging. It was a classic Category Two response: A security worker was fired.

Remember that this passenger carried a gun on board by accident — and then imagine some concerted effort to carry a weapon through the screening point.

Well, no need to imagine. A few weeks after 9/11, a screener detected that a passenger was carrying two knives. They were confiscated and the passenger was allowed to continue up to the boarding gate. The problem: He was carrying seven other knives, a can of tear gas, and a stun gun. Officials were fast to announce an even stronger Category Two response than just firing a security worker: This time, they fired several.

Presumably, somebody thought that would help solve the problem. And yet four days later, a passenger in Florida got on board an international flight even though he was carrying . . . knives and a stun gun.

Incidents of passengers carrying weapons through the screening process have been happening nonstop for thirty

years, and yet people ask incredulously, "How could someone get through with a gun?" We should be more incred-
ulous about the expectation that it would never happen.
You can make the existing workers into federal employees,
you can double their salaries, you can provide high-back
leather chairs and frequent massages, you can staff the
X-ray machines with members of Congress — and you
will still regularly have human error in this job that is both
complicated and hypnotically boring at the same time.

Many believe that X-ray machines flag weapons in
some way. They don't. The process relies entirely on visual
inspection of a one-dimensional view of the contents of
carry-on bags. Some machines have a system called E-scan
that color-codes different elements so that it's easier to tell
metal from organic materials such as fabric and paper and
leather. A handgun might or might not be positioned in
such a way that a perfect profile of the shape is visible. It
might or might not be blocked by other metal objects; it
might or might not be fully assembled — and on and on.
It isn't possible for X-ray screeners to do the job perfectly,
and eventually we will run out of people we can fire to
soothe our anxieties. Should we tolerate laziness or negli-
gence? Of course not. But should we expect superhuman
powers? Not unless we want to be disappointed.

To be clear, weapons screening has been effective at detecting thousands of firearms, almost all carried by people
who had poor memories (forgot they had the guns) but
had no sinister intent (were not hijackers). I support
weapons screening of airline passengers, but I oppose blind
reliance upon it. It is both a Category One and Category

Two precaution, implemented decades ago to stop anxiety about flying and to stop hijacking. It did for a time stop anxiety. It did not stop hijacking. In fact, all of the deaths associated with airline hijacking in America have occurred *since* we instituted weapons screening. So, it's clear that's not where our safety salvation lies.

Do the searches, of course. Do them as well as possible, but recognize that the true solutions are elsewhere. Put plainly, it's possible to improve one door on each aircraft and make it nearly perfect; it is not possible to get anywhere near perfection with one billion passenger screenings a year.

There's another aspect of old thinking we'll benefit from letting go of: The current screening system is aimed at detecting firearms, and to a lesser and less reliable extent, bombs. We learned on September 11 that firearms and bombs are not required equipment for successful hijackers. We must honor the reality that anyone can board a flight carrying a knife made of wood, carbon, bone, fiberglass, plastic, resin, and on and on. None of the detection systems currently in use can address any of these materials, and anyway, the weapons themselves don't even matter that much.

The main weapons of the 9/11 hijackers were determination, ruthlessness, and small cutting instruments that would not likely have been detected through screening. Once in the cockpit, persons of sinister intent could lock the door and incapacitate the pilots with or without weapons. There are so many examples of dangerous things a person could do that one is limited only by the imagination.

Caustic liquid in the eyes, even liquor that is served on board, could be enough to render pilots unable to fly, if even for a short time. That can mean a perfect terrorist success because the airliner can be taken out of stable flight by tampering with the major controls. Flying takes some training and skill — crashing takes none at all.

I mentioned that some of this chapter would be disturbing, but here's the good news about the passenger-screening problem: It's not that big a problem. Why? Because if you have appropriately fabricated and secured doors, and you keep them closed throughout the flight, it doesn't matter so much what a passenger carries on board.

BATHROOM USE BY PILOTS

In the future, aircraft may be modified or built to have bathrooms within the cockpit space, though the vast majority won't have that enhancement for many years to come. In the meantime, some airlines have implemented this procedure for bathroom trips: A pilot calls a flight attendant, who determines that the area around the cockpit is free of passengers. The pilot looks through a viewer to confirm that it's safe before opening the door. The flight attendant enters and the pilot exits at the same time. *The pilot does not have a key for re-entry.* When the pilot returns from the bathroom, the flight attendant confirms through the viewer that nobody else is around, opens the door — and they trade positions.

This works fairly well because it means that when the cockpit door is locked, there is never anybody outside with a key. The only way someone can get in is by being admitted by someone who is already inside.

A better access system would be to install an inexpensive concealed camera and microphone so the pilots can remotely view and monitor sounds in the area around the cockpit. (Some airlines have done this voluntarily.) When satisfied that it is safe to do so, the pilot who remains in the cockpit would be able to unlock the door remotely to readmit the pilot who has left to use the bathroom.

STOP IN-FLIGHT MEAL SERVICE FOR PILOTS

In-flight meal service for flight crews is a luxury, not an aviation requirement. Assuming that cockpit doors are properly improved, meal service poses *the single most substantial advantage to hijackers — and the single greatest security risk to the rest of us.*

The solution can be stated simply:

> Stock the cockpit with pre-flight meals and drinks to reduce the number of times the pilots must open the door.

These meals can be made fancy, creative, even luxurious. As a longer-term solution, airlines could develop a tray pass-through slot in the door or elsewhere in the wall of the cockpit.

You might wonder what difference it makes if the door is opened for meal service, since it has to be opened anyway for trips to the bathroom. Well, first of all, there's just the sheer number of openings associated with food and beverage service. Between taking the meal orders, delivering the trays, picking up the trays, snacks, dessert, coffee, grapes and cheese, there's an average of *fifteen* unnecessary openings per five-hour flight. One jetliner pilot recently told me, "The flight attendants who are best liked are the ones who come in and offer you coffee early in the flight — and keep the food coming the whole trip."

Second, unlike bathroom trips, meals occur at fairly predictable times. Third, when the door is opened for a bathroom trip, the pilot is standing and facing the doorway, a far better position to detect and repel an intruder. Any struggle or challenge that occurs right at the door cannot last long, because cabin crew and passengers will address it. But if an intruder succeeds at getting in quickly during meal service, and locks the door behind him, then the improved locks actually work against air safety — by defeating the in-flight security system that most effectively protects airliners against hijacking: the passengers.

WHAT YOU CAN DO

There are many aspects of airport and airline security that I have not explored in this chapter, either because they are handled effectively or because they are still being studied and improved by government. What I have presented are enhancements and procedural matters that have been mostly missing from the public dialogue. I have focused upon enhancements you personally can influence through communicating with government and, perhaps most effectively, through your patronage of airlines that most closely adopt the philosophies we've explored. You vote, in effect, with your travel dollars, and so far, no security expert, aviation expert, or pilot has been able to tell me a single good reason to continue flight-attendant meal service into cockpits. The first airline to curtail it will get my patronage, to be sure.

Military jets scrambled to fly alongside passenger planes, National Guard personnel at the airports, lengthy searches on the ground, and all the dialogue in all the congressional hearings will not add up to the effectiveness of the eight simple improvements suggested in the letter proposed below. I invite you to send it to the President, with copies to the FAA, your senators, your congressional representatives, and the major airlines. (If you use e-mail, the letter text and e-mail addresses are provided at my firm's Web site.)

Dear Mr. President:
I appreciate that you are working hard to help get the American public comfortable about flying again, and I know you are exploring several enhancements to airport and airline security. I want to share with you those precautions that would be particularly relevant to my feeling safest when flying commercially:

1. Fabricate and install cockpit doors that are truly bullet-resistant, to replace the temporary fixes that were undertaken in 2001.
2. Install locking systems that make the doors truly entry-resistant, to replace the temporary fixes that were undertaken in 2001.

3. Install a system that allows officials on the ground to monitor the sounds in the cockpit in the event there is loss of radio contact with the pilots, or a plane off course, etc. (This technology is familiar to millions of drivers who have On-Star and comparable services.)
4. Have a video and audio system that allows pilots to observe and listen to the area outside the cockpit. Equipment cost: $1,500
5. Have a remotely operable access system that pilots can use from within the cockpit. Equipment cost: $2,000
6. Make the issue of cockpit security part of the pre-flight safety instructions, with words to the effect that "protection of the cockpit door is a duty of both crew and passengers."
7. Prohibit in-flight meal service if it requires opening the cockpit door.
8. Require pilots to keep cockpit doors closed and locked at all times there are passengers on board.

Mr. President, if you accomplish these things, we passengers (along with the cabin crews and occasionally helped by air marshals) will do the rest.

Sincerely,

THE MOST RELIABLE SECURITY SYSTEM

Everyone who has ever planned or undertaken a hijacking knew that controlling the passengers was a top priority. But today, whatever hijackers say, whatever they do, passengers will not willingly participate. This was proved during the Greyhound bus incidents when passengers immediately and powerfully subdued attackers who placed everyone's safety at risk. It was proved again on an American Airlines flight heading to Chicago less than a month after the 9/11 hijackings. A man yelling about crashing the plane into the Sears Tower bashed through the door and entered the cockpit. The pilot pushed him back — but didn't have to do much else because literally on the man's heels there was a posse of passengers who subdued him immediately.

Were the passengers hesitant? Not at all. I interviewed one, Bill Neff, who intervened even though he thought at first that several people were charging the cockpit. (He saw the cockpit intruder and those chasing him.) He put it clearly: "The rules have changed."

Well, most of the rules have changed, but there's a few left to change still, and once they're done, the passengers will get the main thing we need from the FAA right now: Just a few seconds of cockpit entry resistance during which we can respond.

There are those who'd rather leave responding to an air marshal, but I don't find the air marshal program to be quite the solution it is held out to be.

President Bush quickly responded with a plan implying that air marshals will be on every flight. Many Americans were relieved, but it was just a plan — and one that's not likely to happen. Given that we have thirty thousand commercial flights each day, an air marshal on every flight would require creating one of the nation's largest law-enforcement agencies. Even were that the best use of our resources, it can't happen quickly. And even if it could, an air marshal isn't likely to be more effective than the combined will and intervention of regular passengers. Further, passengers may incorrectly assume that an air marshal is on board, and thus hesitate to act if needed. Like many security proposals floated to soothe fear, this one might make things slightly less safe.

As I said in the first chapter, hijackings of the type we have experienced over the past forty years are over. That form of terrorism has been defeated by the lowest-tech security system: the passengers' acceptance of reality and responsibility.

I'm sure you embrace the argument that fifty or a hundred passengers can easily subdue one or two people trying to get into the cockpit. But what if you've never seen yourself in the role of physically taking on another person? The good news is you don't have to. There are plenty of recruits on board every flight, and you might make a different contribution to safety, like my friend Carrie does.

Carrie is a frequent flyer who was understandably afraid about air security after 9/11. She now assesses all the passengers she sees prior to boarding (as you likely do as well). She pays attention to anything that triggers her intuition (as you likely would). For example: two people who aren't traveling together and yet who seem to be communicating in some way, people who are adjusting items under their coats, people who seem uncommonly anxious, people who are suspicious in ways that you can't even explain, etc. Carrie is not shy about making a report to airline personnel.

But Carrie's biggest contribution to air safety is that she selects athletic and capable-looking passengers who are waiting in the boarding lounge and introduces herself, asking, "Are you a Let's Roll-er?" meaning, are you someone who would intervene in the event of an onboard problem? She has found that people are happy to talk and are reassuring. Carrie's fear of hijackers is gone, because by the time she boards, she has a squadron of convivial but effective protectors who have met one another, talked about strategy, and pledged themselves to a highly unlikely but very serious mission.

There's something wonderful about knowing that brand-new friends can be so reliable. Fly happily, because you are already flying more safely than at any time in your life.

8

NO NEWS AT ELEVEN

And Five Other Ways to Be Armored Against Terror

O N FRIDAY, OCTOBER 12, 2001, NBC *Nightly News* anchor Tom Brokaw found himself in the middle of all the anthrax stories. For once, he was not reporting only on the travails of others — he had a personal story to tell America. His own assistant, Erin O'Connor, had apparently contracted an anthrax skin infection — nonlethal, but very unpleasant, and no doubt a sad experience for her and her family, and for Brokaw.

Brokaw devoted a large percentage of the telecast to what had happened, and almost 5 percent of the program talking about his feelings in the matter. He noted that the situation had forced him to move studios and that it was "so unfair and so outrageous and so maddening, it's beyond my ability to express it in socially acceptable terms."

How could this happen? Where in the world could someone have found anthrax? And even if a person knew where it was, how could he get it? And even if a person obtained it, how could he deliver it?

Good questions. Good enough that NBC had been giving Americans detailed answers on these subjects for some time. The very same day of Brokaw's calamity, one NBC News story offered this: "As many as five hundred labs in the United States store samples of anthrax and other biological agents. Access is restricted, but not foolproof." It went on to provide the name of an easy-to-find organization "that lists four hundred seventy-two members in sixty-one countries where labs store anthrax and other deadly agents." The story quoted an expert who said theft was a good way to obtain anthrax because nobody would "necessarily be able to see if someone took it from the laboratory." Still not finished, it included three quite excellent suggestions as to how a "dedicated individual" could get anthrax, while another NBC News story provided four more great ideas.

I am not repeating the tips for acquiring anthrax here, a choice that Erin O'Connor — and maybe even Brokaw — might now agree with. (I'll come back to the issue of disclosing dangerously detailed information at the end of this chapter.)

On the day Erin's infection was confirmed, the NBC News Web site opened with the guaranteed-to-frighten image of a man in a gas mask, and a story called "Anthrax Concerns Spread Across U.S." Some of the nation's concern no doubt resulted from these NBC News reports: "Anthrax, Never out of Reach," "Preparing for Terror," "Anthrax Vaccine Limitations," "Anthrax Alarm," "Mankind's Weapons of Terror," "Hospitals Ill-Prepared."

In case there was one resilient American left who wasn't yet scared nearly to death, NBC broadcast this distorted warning: "Two hundred pounds released upwind in Washington, D.C., could kill three million people." The word *released* implies something clawing to get out of its cage and go kill people, when the truth is that most of the imaginary two hundred pounds of anthrax would fall to the ground and most of the supposed victims would be indoors anyway. Maybe if all 3 million people volunteered to go out and scoop the spores into their mouths, NBC's ambitious estimates could be accomplished — but absent that, the exaggerated report amounts to nothing more than an advertisement to extremists and madmen, and electronic terrorism for the rest of us.

NBC ran some anthrax stories under the logo AMERICA STRIKES BACK. The more appropriate logo would have been AMERICA STRIKES AMERICA, because that's what's going on when our own TV news terrorizes us.

It seems to me that broadcast news is of greatest service when it tells us what has happened and what is happening now, not when it makes up stories about what might happen or could happen in some awful version of the future. Those stories are not predictions assembled with some science: they are the electronic equivalent of jumping out of the bushes in the dark and startling us.

Without making judgments about this, let's acknowledge that the news business is a business. It seeks to balance its stated mission of informing the public against its sometimes more compelling mission of competing with others in the same business. The rush to be first appears to have eclipsed the rush to be accurate. You can always speculate now and clean it up later. Language, images, and graphics are carefully chosen toward the goal of getting around our natural editing by making each story seem urgent or significant or new. One result is that many viewers are left swimming in pictures of fear rather than with a balanced perspective on the situation as it stands.

For example, when Tom Brokaw was interviewed on another NBC News show after his assistant contracted the treatable skin infection, he said he'd be taking antibiotics, and in just the kind of sound bite you'd expect from a seasoned newsreader, he described his experience as "the ultimate nightmare." That doesn't leave much hyperbole for the kinds of things he warns will happen to the rest of us, does it?

When asked on the *Today* show if he felt the tainted letter was tied to the 9/11 terrorist attacks, Brokaw replied, "I think that it would not be appropriate of me to speculate." That is the only time I ever heard anyone in TV news reluctant to speculate, and Brokaw went further: "We just have to stay focused on what we know and not what we don't know." If you start tugging on that thread, the whole fabric of TV news will unravel, because focusing on what is not known is precisely what newsreaders and their producers do most of the time, applying the tools of their trade: speculation, supposition, rumor, gossip, projection, and conjecture.

Having anthrax spores blown into our imaginations, we would, predictably, want to know about treatment and vaccination, and the NBC News anchors had the answers, presented for maximum anxiety: The vaccine, they reported, "is not highly effective, and there were a number of people who were vaccinated that subsequently developed anthrax." They also warned that, "Only one laboratory in the country is capable of producing the vaccine." Antibiotics work, of course, but Brokaw reminded us of what he called "an acute shortage of Cipro." Actually, we'd have an acute shortage only if we had mass contamination, just as we'd have a shortage of water if it all dried up — but these things are not happening.

Having squeezed anthrax for all its fear value, they switched to other biological scourges, describing in detail how each could attack our bodies. Finally, they resurrected the two plagues — pneumonic and bubonic — and called them "history's most feared contagious diseases." That would seem a good time to tell viewers that bubonic plague is not, in fact, at all contagious human-to-human. They might also have explained that plague was "history's most feared" disease because during much of history there were no antibiotics.

The network's on-air medical expert, Dr. Bob Arnot, was, interestingly, the most subdued (and least broadcast; his comments were removed from their Web site in favor of another medical expert). Dr. Arnot described anthrax skin infection as "not that big a deal in terms of an illness. It's usually recognized . . . it's easily treated with antibiotics, it is not spread from one person to another, it is not a major public-health concern."

Despite this, NBC employees were understandably concerned and afraid when they learned that someone within the company had contracted an anthrax skin infection. NBC executives reacted quickly to soothe the fears of its own employees. An internal memo from the two top people quickly assured employees this was "NOT the same respiratory anthrax that has been reported on the news."

Contrary to the rapid spread that NBC News has warned us of so many times, the calming corporate executives wrote: "We have no reason to believe that this particular incident has spread beyond this individual employee." They added: "She is in no danger, and she should recover fully and completely."

While NBC News was telling the public that a letter mailed on September 25 definitely contained anthrax, the cooler-headed executives reassured employees that the letter had been tested by the Department of Health, the Centers for Disease Control, and the FBI, and added that "all these tests came back negative." It turned out that another letter, found later, did test positive for anthrax. The confusing exercise was hopefully instructive for these executives who were forced to deal with the ever-changing alarm of the TV news — just like the rest of us have to deal with it.

But how were these businessmen so calm? Hadn't they seen NBC's warning about a strain of anthrax "so lethal, just eight gallons could kill everyone on earth"? If you could get your hands on that stuff, you wouldn't even need the list of targets suggested in another NBC story: "air bases, ports, key infrastructure installations, oil and power facilities, desalination plants, and civilian population centers." You could just kill everybody on earth, like they said. (Given Brokaw's understandable outrage about his own experience, imagine how mad he'd be if someone killed everybody on earth.)

Seriously, Tom (and Peter and Dan and every other respected TV newsperson), I know that terrorism in America is new to you, too, and you are still getting your bearings. But you can make a huge difference here: Encourage your employers and your peers to stop providing information in a way that is itself hurtful to the general public — and is helpful to our dangerous enemies. Tom, in your excellent interview with Director of Homeland Security Ridge, you said, "We've had a good life. Are young Americans going to have a lifetime of fear?"

You can do more than just pose the question. You can help change the answer.

∎ ∎ ∎

While I have focused on NBC to make several points, CBS News is also a member of the Frequent Frighteners Club, with its own poor record, including the admonition that Iraq has "approximately three times the amount [of anthrax] needed to kill the entire current human population by inhalation." No word from CBS News on how such inhalation could be accomplished, though their Web site does have a clever interactive diagram of the human body with the instruction to "Click the spots to find out how inhaled anthrax spores can kill."

The CBS News Web site offers stories about anthrax under the heading EXPERIENCE THIS STORY. Why would we want to experience it? In stark contrast to their silly Web site is a comment made by Dan Rather after an employee in his office tested positive for anthrax. Very much to his credit, he said, "Our biggest problem today is not anthrax. Our biggest problem is fear."

Proving Rather's point is Fox News, where I recently saw an interview with an expert on "nuclear terrorism" (an interesting expertise, considering there's never been an act of nuclear terrorism). It just wasn't scary enough, I suppose, so correspondent E. D. Donahey first proposed a viable way for terrorists to get around the difficulty of obtaining nuclear material, and then said, "I'm not giving anyone any ideas they don't already have in their sick minds, but what if they blew up a nuclear device in Times Square?" Fox calls itself "The network America trusts." That *is* news.

Certainly Fox has the most anxiety-producing style of the major networks. Their stories soar on wings of melodrama, with montages that look like action films, pounding bass drums, panicky musical scores, striking visual effects, and urgent-seeming sound cues, as viewers are flashed from correspondent to correspondent.

At the other end of the spectrum is ABC, the network that, in my opinion, takes the most reasoned and constructive approach to news — and not a single interactive death game on their Web site. Often, my personal choice has been CNN, for a few reasons. Being on twenty-four hours a day, they have less time pressure, less need to impose false urgency into every minute, and less direct competition during hours that other major channels are broadcasting entertainment.

National news is frightening enough, but there's nearly forty hours a day of local TV news produced in every major city — and that's where the fear tactics are field-tested.

If you detect some disdain on my part, it isn't for the people who read the news; I like and respect many of them, just as you probably do. (Brokaw himself has made some compassionate contributions when out from behind that desk — through his writing.) My disdain is for the choices made by people who produce the TV news. Every word you hear spoken is another choice, every image, every color — all choices. Combine the words, the graphics, the logos, the music, the urgency, and what you end up with is information hidden behind sensation — and the sensation is fear.

Having dedicated my life to helping people put fear in its natural place, it's hard to watch the country be so undone by unnecessary anxiety. Further, the folks who put on the news can do such an excellent job, as they did on September 11 and the days that followed. Those events defied exaggeration. All the newsreader had to do was get out of the way and let us see the images. The stories didn't need to be spiced up ("a tidal wave of dust . . ."). Newsreaders directly and plainly shared the information they had, because those tragedies were, for once, enough just the way they were.

Now that we have lived through the previously un-thinkable, our minds are more open to the unfathomable — and television news has rushed through that opening. They feed our hunger to anticipate what's coming next with worst-case scenarios and dark predictions for the future, as if those outcomes were logical next steps. Many are not logical next steps. Seeing detail heaped upon detail, watching sober experts validate the wildest of conjectures, viewing footage of locations and hearing step-by-step descriptions of how each doomsday outcome might play out, the audience is left with vivid pictures that take our worst fears a step further than we had likely imagined. With such strong imagery filling our minds, the qualifying words ("might," "allegedly," "unconfirmed," "possibly," "could," "potentially," "conceivably") drop from our consciousness, leaving only the sense that danger is everywhere around us.

Since there can't be a video of what isn't happening, they show us the terrifying footage of a similar incident five years ago. If there were no survivors in a tragedy, they show us an interview with a psychologist who speculates about "their final moments." If nothing like it has ever happened in the history of the planet, they show us an animated version, such as the story days after the last Los Angeles earthquake: "Next up, what would have happened if a tidal wave had been caused by the earthquake!," and an animated depiction of blue washing over downtown Los Angeles (I swear to God).

Even before the various anthrax incidents and reports (fewer incidents than reports, of course), 30 percent of Americans feared foreign viruses. I actually met a woman with that fear, by the way. I met her, predictably, in a TV news studio. The station was doing a special segment on a lethal new disease virtually certain to kill us all before the end of sweeps week: the flesh-eating disease. Lacking anyone who actually suffered from the malady, the news producer brought in a woman who feared she *might* have it.

I was introduced to her in the hallway as she headed to the studio, and we talked for a moment. As I watched her interview, it crossed my mind that she could have told me all this *before* shaking my hand.

But no matter, she didn't have it, and I didn't catch it, and neither will you. This story followed a common template of TV news: One person in a distant location contracted a horrific disease. Someone gave it a name so vivid that it lodged in our minds, a horror story come to life. The appearance of a woman who thought she might have contracted the disease allowed the local station to replay the footage of the unfortunate individual who really did have it, along with warnings from the experts who commented on it. And while the woman I met was never afflicted, the enduring thought burned into the memories of audience members was that flesh-eating bacteria *have come to your neighborhood!*

Whenever I think about the flesh-eating disease, I hear the words of the television news producer who told me: "A little worry never hurt anybody."

But in fact, anxiety kills more Americans each year than all the foreign viruses, electromagnetic fields, airplane crashes, and blown-up buildings put together — through high blood pressure, addiction, heart disease, hypertension, depression, and all the other stress-related ailments.

With all the risk and danger they bark at us, the news

should simply open each evening's show by saying: "Welcome to the Channel Two News; we're surprised you made it through another day. Here's what happened to those who didn't."

■　■　■

Think of the times your mind just wouldn't stop chewing on something, just couldn't stop tossing and turning in its own bed of nails, just couldn't find peace. Recall your worst times in the mind and understand that the TV news is that exact same energy given a billion dollars in resources, wired to propel itself far and near, inspired to dwell on every fear, and nurtured as it spins around the world until it reaches terminal velocity.

The news media is a giant mind, a giant unquiet, overstimulated mind that won't let itself rest — and won't let the rest of us rest.

If you had a friend who treated you the way TV news has treated you — calling every twenty minutes barking about a new emergency drama — you'd change your number. But when a national news anchor does it with his weighty intonations, we actually volunteer. It's a vast game of telephone, an unleashed gossip virus: "I heard that Saddam Hussein said that he knew a Muslim extremist whose cousin dated an Afghan woman who worked at the hospital where Richard Gere . . ."

In millions of homes, the newscaster is a guest who arrives in the afternoon full of frightening tales and gory pictures. He stays through dinner, enthusiastically adding grisly details that make the kids wince, and he's still around at bedtime to recite a scary story or two. While he's showing the slides of his awful vacation, you slump to sleep, only to find in the morning that he is still there, eager and fast-talking, following you around the kitchen, warning you about the dangers of coffee. If it weren't for the fact that occasionally he says something that's actually important, you'd throw this guest from Hell out your house.

Now, for a moment imagine that, unlike the unquiet mind, this nightmare could be easily switched off. That peaceful thought brings me to five guidelines for a happier and safer life in the age of terrorism.

TERROR-FREE GUIDELINE #1

Turn off the sensational, uninspirational, uneducational, privacy-meddling, death-peddling, celebrity-snooping, helicopter-swooping, flesh-eating, rumor-repeating, minicam-toting, fear-promoting TV news.

If we turn it off, then we can face the important question, which is not how we might die, but rather, How shall we live? And that is up to us.

(This same suggestion applies even more so to your children. See Appendix B for other guidelines about how to talk to your children about terrorism.)

TERROR-FREE GUIDELINE #2

Keep the TV news off at least long enough to see — as you will — that you're not missing anything, and that you are feeling happier, more courageous, more connected to the people you've chosen to have in your life, and, perhaps surprisingly, better informed.

TERROR-FREE GUIDELINE #3

Get your information in print. Read.

Stay informed by reading. Read *Time* magazine, or *U.S. News & World Report,* or *Newsweek,* or the newspaper. If you feel there's an emergency (and you make that decision yourself as opposed to being told by some newsreader), put on CNN or even the local news for *one telling* of the story. You won't miss a thing — unless you miss feeling anxious.

Why is reading so much healthier than watching the news? When you read something, you decide how scary or alarming or calming it will be. You get the information, but you decide what it will look like to your soul. Your intuition can consider it without the distraction of an elevated heart rate. If you really want to see the buildings fall down again, okay, but if you don't, you don't have to.

When you read what someone has written, you get the benefit of that person's having had a second to take a breath, a moment to think. TV news personalities are chattering all the time, they're watching the same freeway chase you are, they don't know any better than you if that driver who won't pull over for police is a madman or just someone who hasn't looked in the rearview mirror yet. But unlike you, they have to keep talking, keep asking the pilot of Chopper Six if he thinks the driver could have links to suspected terrorist mastermind Osama bin Laden.

Unlike when you watch the TV news, when you read what someone has written, you don't see what they edited out, you don't have to see the thoughts they thought better of and rejected. You don't have to absorb what will be outdated just a minute from now, when the TV newsreader reporting on the overturned oil rig on the freeway wishes he hadn't said, "This is reminiscent of the Bhopal, India, disaster where thousands died from a chemical leak."

TERROR-FREE GUIDELINE #4

Get information — don't let information get you.

If you're interested in something, do research. Check the Internet, read about it, go to a library, look at a Web site, ask a smart friend — but don't let some TV newsreader tell you what's important. Be willing to miss the gossip of "developing stories" and wait for the perspective and caution of the newsmagazines. (See Appendix A for a list of suggested resources. This list is also provided on my firm's Web site.)

TERROR-FREE GUIDELINE #5

Talk to people in your life about world and local events. TV news imitates human interaction, right down to the chummy banter, when in fact it is preventing human interaction. Television connects you to nothing except the illusion that you are connected to something. By contrast, you can be connected to your friends, family, neighbors, co-workers; talk with them about events, and thus get your emotions out, get your feelings felt, get clarity and perspective; in short, bring real life into your life, as opposed to being a cog in a for-profit business that nurtures and feeds upon your anxiety.

■ ■ ■

Finally, a word about national security and the news: Knowing something of how acts of violence are conceived and planned, I want to speak for a moment strictly from a security point of view about the kind of information the TV news provides too much of. To harm America, an enemy abroad or an enemy within the country needs to do little intelligence work today. A TV news story profiles the Arizona firm that has the nation's largest sample of anthrax. Here is the name of the company, here is the outside of their building, and here are the two owners talking away, giving a tour of the inside of their facility.

Nobody in America will shut up.

Pick a target, and here are its inner workings, here's the guy who runs the place, here's a diagram, here it is from the air. We provide our appreciative enemies with things they could never afford to get on their own, like aerial photos of Hoover Dam, for example. We don't give just the list of targets, we provide the intelligence information about each one ("How Utilities Are Beefing Up Security").

News reports advised us that the letter containing anthrax that was sent to Brokaw on September 16 had no return address. The criminal paid attention, and by

October 9, the letter he sent to Senator Daschle did have a return address.

After offering leads to hundreds of places where mad-men could find anthrax, the TV news then said there was only one lab that could produce the vaccine — a critical place for Americans right now — and they identified the place and broadcast images of the actual building!

Many intelligent folks will make the argument that this is a free country and that Americans want to know. But what do we really want to know?

Do we want to know every frightening thing that could befall us? And do we want to then chew on each frightening outcome to the point where we might as well have experienced it happening? If a thing hasn't happened, if it is not happening now, do we really want to live each nightmare within our collective imaginations?

Maybe the answer to these questions used to be yes, but somewhere in our shared experience of terrible things, there is an opportunity for Americans to reconsider our old role in the news business.

Terrorists seek publicity, the media seek stories, and the rest of us seek shelter from uncertainty. We know that for each unlikely risk we react to, we take on another risk: the risk of being governed by fear. Unwarranted fear is its own tyranny, and every day we bow to it, we move further from the freedom we fought our earliest war to get — and fought several other wars to defend.

· 9 ·

THE NEWSSPEAK OF FEAR

Television has its good side and its bad side.
The good side is, it makes dictatorship impossible.
The bad side is, it makes democracy unbearable.

— SHIMON PERES

I T WOULD BE INTERESTING if the standards of Truth in Advertising were applied to television news as they sometimes are to television commercials. In that unlikely situation, TV news writers would be required to use phrases and words that convey accurate information — as opposed to the phrases and words they use today.

I want to help you break the code of alarming newsspeak so that you can more easily find the valuable information that may (or may not) be part of a story.

Given the disturbing reasons we've all been watching so much TV news, it would be understandable to overlook the sheer ridiculousness that is inherent in some of the sensationalism. Occasionally, the way TV news is delivered can be downright funny, and, indeed, the ability to laugh at something indicates that we are beginning to gain perspective on it. Accordingly, some of what follows is funny, and I have a very clear purpose in offering it: I want to help change your experience of television news, to help you actually watch it differently. I want to provide some tools you can use to ensure that when you watch TV news, only actual information gets through.

Though this glossary is not offered as comprehensive, here are some examples of words and phrases I think you'll quickly recognize.

"POSSIBLE"

As in, "Next up, possible links between Saddam Hussein and tooth decay."

The word "possible" doesn't really have the specificity one hopes for in journalism, given that it is completely accurate when applied to anything anyone can possibly imagine. "A possible outbreak of . . ." means there has been no outbreak. "A possible connection between memory loss and the air you breathe . . ." means there is no confirmed connection.

"Officials are worried about possible attacks against . . ." means there have been no such attacks.

Anytime you hear the word *possible,* it's probably not happening right now.

LINKS

"Next up, possible links between convicted murderer Charles Manson and yesterday's traffic jams in the downtown area."

Are these two things linked? Absolutely, if you loosen your criteria enough. Everything is linked by its presence on the same planet with everything else at the same moment in time — but only a very few links are instructive or meaningful.

Links are a great news trick, because you can tie a remote, unconfirmed, or even unimportant story to something that's really pushing buttons. "Next up, possible links to bin Laden" is all you have to say to get attention these days.

Almost always when you hear the word *link,* there is no confirmed link.

"OUR NATION'S"

"Our nation's water supplies," "Our nation's roadways," "Our nation's shipping ports."

Phrases like these are used to imply some large scale to a story. "A new threat to our nation's water supplies" won't be a threat to our nation's anything. Our nation is enormous. Nothing, not even nuclear bombs, poses a threat to all of any system in our society at the same time. When they say "our nation's" anything, they are usually trying to give grand significance to something that doesn't have grand significance. We might not perk up as much if they said, "A new threat to Klopp County's water supply." A story about old Doc Ames's truck leaking oil into the reservoir just isn't gonna scare up enough ratings. But this could: "Next up, a new threat to our nation's water supply. An alarming incident that experts say could happen anywhere!"

"SHOCKING NEW DETAILS"

"Shocking new details when we come back."

Well, first of all, the details are not likely to be new, and if they are so critical, why are we waiting till after the commercial, and anyway, what does *shocking* mean at this point? Unless the news anchor reaches through the screen and pulls my hair, I don't imagine he could shock me. They've ruined another word for themselves.

AUDITORS, OBSERVERS, ANALYSTS, INSPECTORS, LOOPHOLES

"Auditors cite loopholes in security at our nation's libraries."

That's right, anytime you have an audit or an inspection, you're going to find something. Auditors are people who've been hired to write reports identifying deficiencies. Have you ever heard of a one-line audit report? "The auditors didn't find one damn thing that could possibly be improved." Did you ever hear of an inspector who said, "We've wasted six months on this inspection, because the place is bloomin' perfect. Whoever's running this show sure thought of everything."

The implication projected in a story about a security loophole is that someone will come crashing through the loophole — but that is not necessarily so. They tell you (and the terrorists) about the loophole because it is frightening, not because it's enlightening.

"IN A CAREFULLY WORDED STATEMENT"

"In a carefully worded statement, the President said . . ."
Is this distinct from those statements that world leaders just
have the kids throw together? "Carefully worded" is often
used to imply that something is being hidden.

"SERIOUS"

"Officials consider the threat to be serious." Is that to dis-
tinguish this threat from the threats they laugh about over
lunch? Taking something seriously does not mean the risk
is great or imminent. It just means officials are doing what
anyone would do.

"Officials here are taking no chances when it comes
to school safety." Sort of. More likely, they're taking no
chances that reporters will broadcast a report accusing
them of taking chances.

"OFFICIALS ARE CLOSELY MONITORING"

This implies that something is imminent, and worthy of
being closely monitored. "Closely monitoring" is like
"Officials are on the lookout for . . ." Both phrases suggest
that something bad is surely coming, as if officials are
standing outside looking around with binoculars.

"COULD," "PERHAPS," "POTENTIAL," "MIGHT"

"NASA reports that a large piece of space junk — perhaps
as big as a freighter — could enter Earth's atmosphere

sometime tonight over North America. Experts warn that it could potentially slam into the earth."

What are we to do with this report? Move a little to the left or right? They don't say, of course, that every night, thousands of pieces of space junk enter Earth's atmosphere and completely burn up before ever hitting the ground, or that no person on earth has ever been struck and killed by a piece of space junk. Or that if something's as big as a freighter before entry, it might end up as small as a grain of sand by the time it reaches the ground — but it *could potentially* hit your house, I suppose.

"AN ALARMING PERCENTAGE"

"Fifteen percent of Americans are at risk of being seriously injured in car accidents on our nation's highways this year."

Whenever you see a percentage cited, reverse it and think about the other share in the equation. For example, from the story above you can conclude that 85 percent of Americans are not at risk of being seriously injured in car accidents this year. Sort of good news, all things considered. Also, phrases such as "a sizable percentage" or "an alarming percentage" can be applied to just about any percentage. Get the actual number, and then you decide if it's sizable or alarming to you.

"AS MANY AS"

"Experts warn that as many as twenty-five thousand people in America may be carrying the deadly gene . . ." or "As many as twenty states may be susceptible to radiation-leakage disasters."

"As many as" means somewhere between zero and the number given.

"IN A DEVELOPING STORY"

A phrase used when they don't really have the story yet.

FORMER EMPLOYEES

"But one former employee at the doomed refinery reveals shocking new information."

What does he reveal? That they fired him because he was too ethical, or because they didn't want to hear the truth? Or that he knew all along? Anyway, he wasn't there the night of the fire, so is he the best source of information? Truth in advertising would require the reporter to say, "We interviewed one man who hasn't been to the refinery in three months — his opinion next."

LANGUAGE FROM ONE STORY BEING USED IN ANOTHER

As certain words and phrases become symbolic or evocative from one type of story, they show up in another. In the days after 9/11 I saw a TV news report about a tropical storm making "a direct hit" on a tiny coastal community, as if the hurricane were aiming. (And the word *tiny* is used because it implies vulnerability. Storms that make direct hits on tiny places are frightening bullies.) A story about a flight that experienced extreme turbulence is headlined TERROR IN THE SKY.

"DEADLY"

As in the popular "deadly virus." This word is used to imply that everyone who gets the virus perishes, when the truth is that very few people die from the virus. If a really serious virus ends up being fatal for 20 percent of the people who contract it, then truth in advertising would require language such as "Next up, a local man is stricken with a highly survivable virus."

It's quite a bit shy of "deadly" when someone tests negative for anthrax, yet in the weeks after 9/11, even a negative test for a "deadly" virus was presented as a frightening thing.

To put this into perspective, flu-related disorders killed 5,000 times as many people as anthrax in 2001. Is anthrax still scary? Yes, and all the more so because of the implication that it was everywhere (colored maps showing the places in the United States where anthrax was found or suspected). It wasn't everywhere. *Reports* were everywhere. And the same report repeated seventy-five times is still the same report. But you wouldn't know that by the excited delivery: "New details emerge in that anthrax case." Details maybe, but not new — far more likely when you watch TV news, they'll be the same "new" details for the tenth time that day.

A storm is described as deadly: "We'll have new information on that deadly hurricane that's heading up the coast."

A hurricane qualifies for the word *deadly* when someone, somewhere, on the hurricane's round-the-hemisphere journey dies as a result of the storm. That does not mean the hurricane tries to kill all people it encounters, but that's the implication — that something dangerous is coming. You'll note that the people who die are usually in a situation far different from yours: They are on a small fishing boat at night off the coast of Peru, and you're at home 1,200 feet above sea level.

"IN A LAST-MINUTE DEVELOPMENT . . ."
"IN A SURPRISE DEVELOPMENT . . ."

These usually mean they didn't get a news crew there in time. Or they didn't warn you about it yet, which actually is interesting, since there are only two or three possible awful outcomes involving human beings that they haven't warned us about yet.

"DISTURBING QUESTIONS"

As in "Disturbing questions have been raised about the safety of our nation's . . ." Yes, the questions are disturbing. They're disturbing everyone. Please stop raising them.

"A NEW STUDY REVEALS . . ." "A NEW REPORT WARNS . . ." "EXPERTS FEAR . . ." "EXPERTS WORRY . . ."

Yes, reports and experts do seem to warn, fear, and worry a lot.

"EXPERTS SAY IT'S JUST A MATTER OF TIME BEFORE . . ."

They sure do.

"BUT NEW YORKERS FEEL . . ."

Global conclusions drawn from man-on-the-street interviews represent literally nothing. You can edit a story into "New Yorkers feel terrified" or "New Yorkers are ready to move on" — it all depends upon which of the five interviews you cut into the piece broadcast.

Here are two quotes brought back by one NBC News crew:

"I think if you change your life, they're winning," says Captain Frank Carver. "So the more we continue our daily routine, the better off we all are."

At Pat's Country Bakery nearby, Joann Charters concedes she's still apprehensive. "It's a really scary feeling with kids in school. You don't know what's gonna happen," says Charters.

To accurately summarize these quotes you'd have to say: "Some people feel one way and some people feel another way. Back to you, Tricia."

Joann Charters citing that it's scary because "you don't know what's gonna happen" is right on. That's why it's scary: because you don't know what's going to happen — not because you do know, not because danger is advancing toward you, *but because it is not.*

TV news stories like this are filler, background, static, irrelevant. You don't need a reporter and a video crew to bring you man-in-the-street opinions. There are men on your street you can get opinions from. Or you could just talk to your friends and family.

WARNING SIGNS

Any list of warning signs implies great risk. I recall a rash of reports about carjacking in Los Angeles, and this list of warning signs:

Armed stranger approaches car;
Taps on closed window;
Looks around suspiciously.

And then they offered the checklist of precautions, given by an "expert on carjacking." (Is there a college course on that?) The checklist:

Keep doors locked;
Don't let strangers into your car;
Drive away.

This is tantamount to: NEXT UP, CRIMINALS WHO HIDE OUT IN YOUR PURSE AND ROB YOU WHEN YOU GET HOME!

Warning signs:
Purse feels extra heavy;
Strange noises coming from purse.

"OFFICIALS ADMIT"

"Officials admit that the incident could have developed into a full-fledged riot." In this context, *admit* means that when a reporter asked, "If police had never reached the scene, and if a hundred other factors had fallen into place in an extraordinarily unlikely way, couldn't this have developed into a full-scale riot?" Yes, it could have — an admission.

EXPERTS

It may seem you are getting expert advice on the news, but that's far from so. The moment an expert's words are edited, they might as well have been put in a blender. Would you let a TV news crew mediate your doctor's advice? Imagine being challenged by a difficult illness and finding that your doctor's compassionate and complete thirty-minute presentation had been edited down to twenty-three seconds.

That's what the local news brings you: expert opinion edited, mediated, and minimized by nonexperts who ask questions designed to elicit the most alarming responses. "Yes, yes, Dr. Stevens, but if it *did* happen, it would be terrible, wouldn't it?"

NAMES, MONIKERS

When the news media assign a nickname to a wanted criminal (e.g., the Night Stalker, the Hillside Strangler) or to a disease (Legionnaire's or flesh-eating diseases), it is indicative of a hoped-for series of reports. When it's a type of crime (follow-home robberies), a trend is not far behind.

For example, freeway shootings and "road rage" led to all these headlines: AGGRESSIVE DRIVERS TURN FREEWAYS INTO FREE-FOR-ALLS, ROAD RAGE: DRIVEN TO DESTRUCTION, HIGHWAY VIOLENCE SPREADING LIKE AN EPIDEMIC.

Next comes "Officials are concerned," and soon enough — as with road rage — you've got hearings before the House Subcommittee on Surface Transportation, and somebody (in this case, committee staff member Jeff Nelligan) calling the issue "a national disaster." Presumably, Mr. Nelligan would tone that down a bit today, all of us having found a new meaning for the words "national disaster."

I TOLD YOU SO

An NBC News story quotes a member of a university task force on weapons of mass destruction: "We've been talking about this for years, and people in general have not been interested." Is there some surprise there — that someone on a task force about weapons would be talking about weapons? The intended implication of these stories is that if someone had just listened, this could all have been prevented. How could discussions at some college task force have been used to prevent anthrax scares? If we had listened, what would be different? This is like an earthquake happening and earthquake experts saying, "We warned you." Yes, you did; you said there'd be an earthquake sometime. If only we'd listened.

DISASTER UNREADINESS

In reporting these stories, TV newspeople cannot lose. They ask hospitals or public-health officials or the utility company or the fire department if they can handle a disaster of X magnitude. If the response is yes, they just keep upping the disaster magnitude until the response is no.

Here's an example from NBC News: "A survey of thirty hospitals in four states and Washington, D.C., found them ill-equipped to handle a widespread biological disaster." A guaranteed fear-inducer, it pokes right at our insecurity. First off, just asking the question implies that a "widespread disaster" is coming, and it's even better if the survey is part of a "new study," because that implies that the question itself is well founded.

Either way, the basic premise of the story is true: If hospitals currently able to handle 500 patients an hour get 5,000 patients in some terrible hour, they will be unprepared. The standard of care will drop. Is there something surprising about that? Do TV newswriters think Americans assume there is some extra team of 200 doctors and an extra 5,000 fully equipped hospital beds waiting in their community somewhere just out of sight?

Indeed, hospitals are unprepared for what they have never had to be prepared. Being able to deal with what predictably comes down the pike and putting your resources where they are most likely to be needed is *good planning*. An emergency room would have to trade some daily-used resource to be ready for mass casualties that don't appear to be coming. Yes, as the world changes and events change, so does preparation — but expecting hospitals to be fully prepared, for example, to treat thousands of inhalation anthrax casualties when there's been just a few lethal cases in thirty years would constitute bad planning.

One can make an "unprepared" story about anything — America's police are unprepared for a "widespread crime disaster"; our supermarkets are unprepared for a "widespread food shortage." It all depends upon how you define the word "widespread." Put a microphone in some official's face and ask if he's adequately prepared for an attack on the harbor by Godzilla, and you've got an unreadiness story.

"WILL NEVER BE FORGOTTEN"

"Being stuck in the elevator for six days is an experience Betty Hamilton will never forget." This is used as a measure of how serious an incident it was, but did anyone imagine she was going to forget it? "I think I was stuck in an elevator for six days, but I can't quite remember."

THE WRAP-UP

Pay attention to the very last line in news reports. They are rarely summaries but rather are designed to keep the story open for more reports. Most often, the closing line takes a last bite at the fear apple, one final effort to add uncertainty and worry. "Many here are left wondering if it will ever be safe," "Fear continues its tight grip on this tiny community," "Whether more will die remains to be seen."

In the world of TV news, frightening stories never end. We never hear the words "And that's that."

.   .   .

Let's put a few of these newsroom strategies together into a story and see how it looks. As the basis for our mock TV news report, I'll draw on something that actually happened to my assistant. Earlier this year, her wrist was injured when a dog bit her.

THE TEASER

"Next up, dogbites! The bone-crushing power of dogs. Experts warn that even friendly dogs can bite, sometimes without provocation. And they're everywhere. A new government study estimates as many as three hundred dogs per square mile, with the numbers climbing each year. How many backyards in your neighborhood are hiding a deadly menace? We'll tell you what experts say — when we come back."

THE STORY

"A shocking bite from the dog everyone described as a little angel leaves one area woman nursing her wounds. Dog-jaw experts say that even a small dog can produce as much as five hundred pounds of biting force, and given the rate at which dogs breed, it's just a matter of time before more people are placed at risk. A former employee with the Department of Health says hospitals are unprepared for a major increase in dogbites, and officials are closely monitoring this situation that could pose a deadly threat to our nation's neighborhoods. Disturbing questions have been raised about loopholes in the licensing system, and observers point out that dogs who bite can receive licenses and be released into neighborhoods."

THE WRAP UP

"It's no surprise that many local residents are living in fear: 'You never know when somebody is walking their dog right behind you. We're scared.' Officials say links between the recent dogbite and one that occurred in the tiny town of Ames, Iowa, have not been confirmed, but either way, it's a nightmare few will ever forget. And one that many fear will not be over in the morning."

■   ■   ■

Coming to understand these popular phrases and strategies, and being able to see around them, has made me appreciate those news reports that are direct, clear, and informative. Since many newspeople use these tricks, those who do not stand out as all the more special and valuable.

If you watch TV news, you're probably going to spot lots of sensationalizing tactics I've missed, and maybe even start a list of your own. If finding them becomes an occasionally enjoyable part of your news-viewing experience, that in itself will be great news.

· 10 ·

FAR FROM THE LIMITS
OF COMPASSION

Me against my brother;
Me and my brother against my family;
Me and my family against my tribe;
Me and my tribe against the world.

— AFRICAN PROVERB

WHEN CHANGE COMES UNINVITED — as it did
on 9/11 — it's not surprising that many people
want things back the way they used to be. I don't. I want
things to be better than they used to be. I believe that
requires us to stay awake. Ironically, remaining awake requires that we get some rest. And real rest requires peace of
mind. Just as with our bodies, our minds are most healthy
when this cycle is completed each and every day: peace
and rest, stimulation and action, peace and rest again.

For us to rest well, everything that torments us about
what happened must be placed in some compartment
within our minds or hearts. In this chapter, I want to
explore our confidence and lack of confidence in law-
enforcement agencies, and discuss what we can fairly
expect from government. But first, there is a question that

still deeply troubles many Americans: What kind of people would do such a thing to us, and why do they hate us so much?

Even the question is instructive, for it calls the perpetrators "people" and not "monsters." Since many think of violence as a mystery, sometimes the greatest contribution I can make to enhance their feeling of safety (and their actual safety) is my refusal to call it a mystery. Rather, violence is a puzzle. I have seen the pieces of this puzzle so often that I may recognize them sooner than some people do, but my main job now is just to get them on the table. Only by understanding those who intensely frighten us do they cease being the omnipotent, alien monsters of our nightmares.

Often we use the word *inhuman* to describe perpetrators of terrible acts, but I know many such people, and they are not inhuman — they are precisely human. Their violent acts were merciless and inhumane, to be sure, but not inhuman.

When a bank robber shoots a security guard, we all understand why; but with something like 9/11, many resist the concept of a shared humanness. That's because *us* and *them* is far more comfortable. But the characterization leaves "them" with power over us, particularly if we call them monsters. As every child knows, monsters are terrifying, overwhelming, relentless, merciless, and nearly impossible to defeat. To call a man a monster is to give him all that — and at the same time to stop understanding him. Scientists, after all, do not observe a bird that destroys its own eggs and say, "Well, that never happens; this is just a monster." Rather, they correctly conclude that if this bird did it, others also might and that there must be some reason, some cause, some predictability.

Though anthropologists have long focused on the distinctions among people, it is recognizing the sameness that allows us to most effectively understand and prevent violence. Accepting someone's humanness does not mean excusing his behavior, of course. This lesson is probably starkest when you spend time with the world's most violent and dangerous people, the ones you might call monsters, the ones who committed acts you might think you couldn't have imagined. Many of them are locked up at Atascadero State Hospital in California, where I visited them several times — to learn. Some of the lessons are explored more fully in *The Gift of Fear,* but for now I want to share the words of a woman who works at Atascadero. After a pet that the patients had cared for died, she wrote to me about what she observed:

> As I sat in my office watching the patients, all felons, many guilty of brutal crimes, most lost in a variety of addictions (you choose), mental illness (pick one), and regarded as the bottom of the barrel, I saw a glimmer of compassion, a bit of emotion, and the glimpse of humanity that society believes these men lack (and in most situations, they do). It is true that the majority of these men are exactly where they belong; to unleash them on society would be unthinkable, but we cannot disregard their humanness, because if we do, I believe, we become less human in the process.

Brutal acts have within them the power to take us to the limits of our compassion; being victimized can lead to our wishing to victimize others. Those sad results are not written in stone, however, and the tragedies of September 11 seem to have brought many Americans to a different place. For example, even while fighting a war in Afghanistan, we have carefully considered the suffering of people who are not our enemies. The military has provided food to the starving, and citizens of the United States and Canada have donated money, time, and services to help people caught in the crossfire. When an American bomb misses its target and accidentally kills an Afghan child, her family must wonder if Americans are monsters. That we care enough — in spite of what happened to us on 9/11 — to hold our government accountable for such accidents is itself a sign of something wonderful in us. And if it is in us, it is in all people.

When I visited ground zero at the World Trade Center, I learned that an Austrian government official was arranging to bring children who had lost a parent in the tragedy to Austria for a visit. That was the first time I had ever heard of foreign aid for American children. When victimized, we were humanized to a world that had never really seen us as subject to the same pains and traumas as the rest of the international community. Truly vulnerable and hurt for the first time, we received compassion from other countries, perhaps also for the first time. As often happens, the worst of human behavior brought forth the best of what people can be.

Are we destined to forever experience such extremes of

cruelty and kindness? In one of history's most remarkable correspondences, Albert Einstein and Sigmund Freud asked the same question, and their answer is yes. Einstein's letter concluded that "man has in him the need to hate and destroy." In his reply, Freud agreed "unreservedly," adding that human instincts could be divided into two categories: "those which seek to preserve and unite, and those which seek to destroy and kill." He wrote that the phenomenon of life evolves from these two instincts (which we could call *love* and *fear*) acting together and against each other.

A Native American parable expresses the truth about us in simpler terms: "Inside of me there are two dogs, one evil and one good. The evil dog and good dog fight all the time. Which dog wins? The one I feed the most." Our individual decision about which dog we shall feed is complicated by the fact that modern humans are the dazed survivors of a continuous, five-million-year habit of lethal aggression. Though we live in space-age times, we still have stone-age minds. In addition to the qualities we can be proud of, we are competitive and territorial and greedy and domineering — Americans and Middle Easterners alike. And we are violent. There are people who insist this isn't so, who insist they could never harm anyone, but they invariably add a telling caveat: "Unless, of course, a person tried to harm my child." Then that peaceful soul would stab, shoot, bludgeon — whatever it might take to protect her child. So the resource of violence is in everyone. *All that changes is our view of the justification.*

At the end of the day, the American bomber who kills a hundred people in Iraq decides to use violence the same way as the Palestinian bomber who kills a hundred people in Israel. Both feel completely justified in doing so.

This idea may bother some readers, but a true understanding of violence requires that we not make value judgments. True understanding requires us to see past politics, past even the seductive concepts of right and wrong — and see straight to the center of our humanness. We must see every battle — at least for a moment — from the deck of the enemy warship, because each person has his own perspective, his own reality, his own justification, no matter how much it may differ from ours. And that brings us back to the question of what kind of people did this to us.

Mohamed Atta and the other 9/11 hijackers were able to act on their personal hatred and desires by stealing justification from the usual suspects: ideology, justice, political belief, religious belief. Throughout history, these have been the most common reasons offered to explain violence — but they never really do explain it.

In recent months we have taken the enormous power of our collective pain and fear and have given it to a new bogeyman: the Muslim fundamentalist, the Middle Eastern terrorist. Oh, some will say, "They are evil, they are far more dangerous than anyone else, they are an adversary as we have never seen before, they are diabolical, brilliant, unstoppable. Sure, we have our own American brand of killer, but these Middle Eastern terrorists are fanatics. After all, they intended to die."

So did the two boys who shot thirty-six people at Columbine High School before committing suicide.

Could it be that the same kinds of motivation that lead to horrific acts by alienated Americans also motivate acts by extremists from the Middle East? Of course.

Yes, he was religious, yes, he was political, but it is also true that Mohamed Atta wanted attention. Not in life, which he couldn't take, but in death. He wanted to be important. He wanted to feel dominant and male. He wanted an identity. He and some of his co-conspirators wanted to feel rich, just like the Americans and Saudis they hated. They hired limousines, drank alcohol, went to strip clubs. Ideology and religion are usually a distant second to the deep desire to right one's personal experience of injustice.

When Atta objected to a $48 bill at a restaurant, the manager asked if he was short of cash. Atta's reply reveals feelings of insignificance that existed long before he embraced someone else's ideology. "No, I have plenty of money," he boasted. "I'm an airline pilot." As he displayed fifty- and hundred-dollar bills, he may have felt important for a moment, but never important enough to the disappointed father who told him, "I need to hear the word 'doctor' in front of your name," the father who thought his son had earned a master's degree in engineering when he hadn't, the father who complained that his son was raised "like a girl" and referred to Atta and his two sisters by telling family members, "I have three girls."

Little surprise that this boy remained awkward with

women his whole life. Little surprise that the man who had few or no intimate relationships on earth was drawn to the promise that his heroism would bring him the affections of beautiful women in heaven. Emasculated Mohamed Atta sought to assert his unasserted maleness through taking on the world's greatest power. Insignificant Mohamed Atta became significant after all.

The same search for significance is part of the motivation for some young gang members who kill, because violence is the fastest way to get identity. Murderer Jack Henry Abbott describes the "involuntary pride and exhilaration all convicts feel when they are chained up hand and foot like dangerous animals. The world has focused on us for a moment. We are somebody capable of threatening the world."

Recall another man who needed to feel capable of threatening the world. When the Unabomber was still at large, each time a new bomb exploded, he was called diabolical, brilliant, unstoppable. He was outsmarting everyone, it seemed — law enforcement could not find him, and we all felt powerless.

When he was finally identified, both *Time* and *Newsweek* pictured Ted Kaczynski on their covers using the word "genius." He was so praised, perhaps, because he flew under the radar for so long; but that's where he lived: under the radar. Once revealed, Ted Kaczynzki was hardly frightening. He was a pathetic man who lived in a shack; he was smelly and lonely, and except for his willingness to kill and maim people by remote control, he was not important to anyone. He assembled bombs, put them in parcels, and mailed them; the Postal Service delivered them, people opened them; some exploded, some didn't; some killed their targets, some didn't. I don't agree that this took genius.

Genius is not behind the acts of September 11, either. Pain is. Cultural pain, historical pain. Certainly, religious ideology, politics, and fanaticism are part of 9/11, and certainly the attacks were acts of war. They were not like more conventional terroristic expressions, designed to draw attention to some cause or plight. September 11 was the choice to pursue destruction that was an end in itself. But it was also about personal pain. I am certain that angry, tense, unhappy, judgmental, intolerant Mohamed Atta was no kinder to himself than he was to us. Just as he hid from everyone else, I am certain he hid from himself, from his own humanness. How do I know? Because as Carl Jung said, "When an inner situation is not made conscious, it appears outside as fate."

Atta may hold the top position on an awful list of mass killers, but he is not unique. He can be understood. Though it may be too early for most of us to think about forgiveness, even Mohamed Atta is not beyond the limits of our compassion. Nobody is. Being compassionate is not something we do for Atta — he is out of this equation. It is something we do in our own interest because humanizing another person is the only route to real understanding. When it comes to an enemy, understanding is required whether we want to forgive him, befriend him, or defeat him.

The question of what kind of people would do hateful things to us begs another question: Who is *us?* And who is *them?*

We're a nation that has had it so good for so long that we nearly forgot there could be adversity on a grand scale. We worry about having enough money in the bank; many people around the world have no such worries, for they have no money and no banks. They hate us for our luxurious worries. We think about getting our kids through school with good grades. Many parents in conflict-torn parts of the Middle East think about getting their kids through childhood alive. Our money in the bank, our medical technology, our insurance, our well-maintained roads, our always-available police, our powerful military that doesn't push us around — these are things we demand. Resources we could not imagine living without are luxuries that most people on earth could not imagine living with.

Why would anyone hate us? Millions of people in the Middle East have spent their lives with the things we experienced for just a few minutes: smoke, rubble, fire, dust, instability, uncertainty, explosions. And the mangled metal a child in Iraq might find when playing in a bombed-out building often has on it something written in English; sometimes it even has our flag on it. As bombs rained down during the Gulf War, Americans went to the mall and out to dinner. Other than a few minutes of interesting video on the evening news, we barely experienced the deaths of tens of thousands of people. By most estimates, Iraq lost more sons and brothers and fathers in twelve weeks than we lost in Vietnam in twelve years, and Iraq is a country with one-tenth our population. We are still suffering from our experience in Vietnam; people are still writing books and songs and movies to work through their pain and bitterness. The people of Iraq are no less wounded or bitter, maybe more so, since they experienced a humiliating defeat by a nation that barely even paid attention.

In the Middle East, it is most often children who make up casualty lists. At the start of our war and subsequent boycott against Iraq, a few hundred children younger than five were killed each month by respiratory infections, malnutrition, and diarrheal illnesses. The shameful number is now more than five thousand — *per month*. In Sarajevo, almost one child in four has been wounded. A UNICEF survey found that more than half of the children in Bosnia have been shot at by snipers, and 66 percent have been in a situation where they thought they were about to die. Over the past decade, about 2 million children have been killed in armed conflicts around the world, more than double that number have been disabled, and more than 12 million have been made homeless — while we worried about tax cuts and interest rates, and who might win an Academy Award.

We have (myself included) been out of touch with most of the people on our small planet. Other people's wars are often little more than geography lessons to Americans.

None of what I am sharing is about right or wrong, or ideology, or politics. I know very well that America contributes enormously to millions of people around the

world, and I am proud of much of what we do. In point-
ing out both sides of our international reputation, I have
just one purpose: to answer the question of why we are
hated by so many. Einstein said, "Peace cannot be kept by
force. It can only be achieved by understanding." Like you,
I want to understand.

America has its own troubles, of course, many of them
very serious, but even on our worst days, most of our
young people were not afraid of being killed — until September 11.

As our hardest times have shown us, people can get
used to great strife, and as our easier times have demon-
strated, people can get used to great prosperity as well.
Americans came to believe that if we could just surround
ourselves with the right walls and moats, just rely upon
government, just spend money on the right things, our
security would be ensured. But all we can get are brief
periods of freedom from insecurity. True security is found
only in the heart. When you long for it, as we all do,
remember that many hearts around the world have been
hardened by lives in which safety is a distant dream — and
they see America as part of their suffering.

From time to time in our future, desperate, envious,
angry, hate-filled men will try to work out their personal
pain on the rest of us. A few will plan acts of enormous
violence. Nearly all of them will fail, as they usually have.
Today, they are even more likely to fail, because now we
are more likely to recognize them before they act. We also
have the makings of a precaution that, if applied early
enough, has the power to make friends of people who

might otherwise have become terrible enemies. That precaution is compassion.

. . .

There's another population that is entitled to our compassion: public officials. They, too, are in a totally new world,
struggling with new risks, new expectations, new rules.
The moment some official disappoints our outrageously
elevated expectations, it seems we forget that we are the
government. That concept isn't just a cliché from our
school days — it is the truth. Today's senior official is yesterday's campaign manager. Don't expect superheroes.

We will feel safer when we abandon the notion that any
government leader is Captain America. As you felt fear of
terrorism, many people in government probably felt more.
It's understandable that mayors and governors and federal
officials were afraid in 2001 — afraid of terrorism, afraid
of making mistakes, and afraid of you. One official we expected perfection from in 2001 was the attorney general,
our top law-enforcement officer, the person who directs
the Justice Department and the FBI. But Attorney General
John Ashcroft, whatever we may feel about his politics, is a
human being, a minister's son whose love of gospel music
led him to become one of the best singers in the Senate.
That's not the background that makes someone an expert
on threats or terrorism or security. He isn't a Green Beret
commando who rappels to work each morning; he is a
man doing the best he can in a situation unlike any he has
ever faced — and that will show from time to time.

The moment we expect humanness is the moment we have a chance to feel surprised and impressed by our leaders. Conversely, our expectations of perfection are merely preplanned resentments, and as long as we hold on to them, we shall continue to be disappointed.

For example, many were disappointed in the CIA and the FBI. They questioned the competence of several agencies after September 11: Where was the CIA? Where was the INS? Why were these hijackers allowed into the country? Isn't the fact that the 9/11 conspirators weren't stopped an enormous oversight on the part of the FBI?

No, it is not. That's the short answer. Though assigning blame is a popular pastime for TV commentators, let's look at this issue with some perspective.

First, assume there is a major bank robbery in Los Angeles or New York City. The police departments in these cities have large intelligence divisions. Still, have you ever in your life heard anyone say, "How could the cops have let this robbery occur? Where were the police? Why didn't they know about it? I mean, the robbers bought the masks just two days before the robbery, right in downtown. They bought two of the guns they used just a week ago. And one of them has a police record! How could the police not have been watching these people?"

Understand that the Los Angeles Police Department is twelve thousand strong, with a jurisdiction covering about 3 million people. The FBI has twelve thousand special agents, and a jurisdiction covering a hundred times as many people as Los Angeles.

You have never heard people blaming the police after

a bank robbery, because our expectations of local police is more reasonable than our expectations of the FBI. The FBI has been so effective at times that Americans expect it be flawless. Flawlessness is not part of humanness, and it certainly isn't part of our criminal-justice system — with its bee's nest of investigative restrictions, civil-liberties issues, and other challenges one doesn't see in movies and TV dramas.

Many major criminal cases are solved as the result of coincidences and unrelated police inquiries. For example, though lots of effective investigative work paid off later, the Son of Sam killer got caught because of a parking ticket. The Unabomber got caught because a relative recognized his handwriting. (It was the FBI's idea to publish his handwriting.) These are cases where crimes had already occurred, but law enforcement's role in stopping crimes before they can occur is far less developed.

Something really hard for some people to absorb in the case of most of the 9/11 hijackers is that even had they been under surveillance in the days and weeks prior to the hijackings, even had they been under surveillance at the very moment they boarded the flight, even had they chanted anti-American slogans the whole way through the airport, law enforcement might not have had grounds to arrest them.

The nature of effective conspiracy is that its core construction is done out of view — and remains out of view until the moment a plan is executed. As with many conspiracies, unless a key insider becomes an informant and provides clear, well-supported information, there is often little reason to assume law enforcement will be able to act decisively.

Also, there is a difference between taking police action to make a case that sticks and police action intended solely to stop a crime. Historically, when crimes were stopped by police action in ways that impeded successful prosecution, there was all kinds of public outcry. We seem to want it both ways: Prevent crime, and get convictions — even though the two goals are often at odds.

Yes, some of the 9/11 hijackers had warrants or other legal grounds for which they could have been detained or even arrested. Mohamed Atta, for example, had a traffic warrant for driving without a license. Had he been arrested, he would also have been released soon after — just as you would be in the same situation. Yes, he had an immigration status that was questionable, and it was questioned at length by immigration officials, who determined that he met the criteria to be readmitted into the country. Had he been arrested on the traffic warrant, and had the questions about his immigration status been pursued again, the result would likely have been exactly the same.

Yes, some of the 9/11 terrorists were added to federal government's watch lists, but they had already entered the United States at that point.

Indeed, in retrospect, we can identify many pieces of information known to the government prior to 9/11 that mean a great deal today. Indeed, there was enough information available to theorize that someone might someday try to fly a jetliner into a building, but I have studied much of what was known to various agencies prior to 9/11, and in the world the way it was then, expecting someone to have put it together and stop all of the planes from being taken is unreasonable.

The United States has a system of criminal justice that intentionally limits the power of law-enforcement investigators. I am not judging it as good or bad, just stating the fact of it. For example, when we think to blame the FBI, recall the case of Zacarias Moussaoui, the man agents arrested after they learned he wanted to learn to fly but not take off or land. Well, agents sought to search his home and conduct other investigative work in August 2001, but they were turned down because it was believed there was not sufficient probable cause for a search warrant. (We Americans care about details like that — a lot.) Much of what we now know about Moussaoui was developed because the second time agents submitted the request to conduct searches, it was granted. Why? Because it was after 9/11, and everyone knew what they knew.

Are there things many agencies could have done better? Could they have worked together more effectively? Absolutely — and we are learning a lot. Could they likely have prevented all the 9/11 conspirators from committing destructive acts? Absolutely not — not the way the world was then.

To put this most starkly, imagine that bin Laden himself had telephoned the *New York Times* on September 10 and said, "Tomorrow my people are going to hijack four commercial jetliners at the exact same time and crash them into both of the World Trade Towers, the Pentagon, and the White House." We still wouldn't have prevented the events from occurring. We wouldn't have taken such a caller seriously. Even if we reacted by placing airline screeners on so-called high alert, it would not have prevented the hijackings. The way things were then, we would not have prevented all Arab-looking passengers from boarding flights, placed federal agents on every plane, or grounded all aircraft in the nation — and that's what it would have taken to be completely assured of safety.

I am certain that law-enforcement officials can act more effectively today and tomorrow than in the past. Why? Because now, nothing is beyond our collective imagination; because now, regular citizens and those in various government agencies are starting to provide the kind of information to law enforcement that can be pieced together in a cohesive way; because now, millions more Americans than ever before are supporting the prevention of violence, which means the options of the FBI and other agencies are already far greater than they have ever been.

I don't advocate that we give blind support to the federal government, and I don't believe any dissent should be silenced. But I do suggest that a climate of cooperative exploration will produce far better results than we'll get with blame and misplaced outrage. In the days following 9/11, I recall a TV commentator angrily interviewing an FAA official: "How in the world did these hijackers get knives on board?" I thought to myself, "Order the steak, and a flight attendant will bring you one." At that time, there were hundreds of knives on board every flight anyway — and it's not as if government had been hiding that fact from us.

With regard to the FAA, most of the people who made decisions that disappoint us today have been gone from the agency for years. Blame doesn't increase safety, and as far as I'm concerned, the current administrators and senior officials of the FAA started with a clean slate on September 11, 2001. Let's work with them to make things better in future Septembers.

Since I've encouraged greater understanding and compassion for our enemies, and for our own leaders, I also want to extend some slack to TV news producers and newsreaders, including the interviewer who was outraged that knives could get on board. She was probably frightened by what had just happened, just like lots of people in the media. Remember, we have to see scary stuff only when we're watching TV news; they have to see it all day.

We've all been through a lot, and many things are different now. Let's keep them different, and not go back to the same divisive, attention-seeking, counterproductive attacks on one another that we'd all gotten so used to. We've got plenty of enemies around the world to think about, and if we take a break from chewing on one another, I think we'll find cooperation to be the most effective route to safety.

■ ■ ■

During my career, I've sat across the table and seen fear in the eyes of public figures, in the eyes of assassins, death-row inmates, soldiers, rape victims, battered women, and police officers. I've discussed fear with a president who was shot at, with another who was hit, with the widow of one who was killed, with an athlete who was stabbed at a sporting event, and with children who grew up surrounded by violence. The fear I've seen has worn a thousand faces, but when unmasked it is the same as yours and mine — and since September 11, we've all seen it at some point in most of the people we've encountered.

Just as we can find compassion for those who hate us and for those who serve in government, so, too, can we find compassion for ourselves. It is just fine that we felt fear, just fine that we canceled some plans, just fine that we didn't know what to do or how to react to a terrible trauma that still seems unreal. Our nation has been terrorized. What we lost at the start of this war was our peace of mind, and it is time to take back that beachhead.

Before we do, there may be some benefit in consciously feeling our fear for just one more moment, because fear can carry us closer to the truth of who we are. When we are frightened, our options multiply enormously. Ideas we might never have entertained are suddenly considered. In that willingness to do things differently resides the opportunity — the privilege — to change our lives in ways we might not have in the absence of fear. Anyone who has beaten cancer or heart disease sees the world differently today than at the moment the doctor sat them down, drew a long breath, and spoke the words that started a new life. You may know such a person. You may be such a person.

For our country, at the exact moment we lost so many lives, we all began new ones. We are changed and changing still, and just as with a person, a nation can become more extraordinary or can slip back into its old ways.

I spoke in chapter 2 about the death of denial. Now I turn to the denial of death. Ernest Becker wrote a Pulitzer Prize–winning book by that title, and a copy of *Denial of Death* lay unopened at my bedside for two years. You could call this denial of denial of death. That I delayed reading that wonderful book was doubly ironic given that my work has always required me to look at the possibility of death, even the architecture of death. Millions of Americans have had to do the same thing since September 11, and many have accepted death and risk in ways they never had before.

This is the same as accepting life, for life is risk; life is a venture full of peril and full of promise. Politicians and the media encourage us to go to war with death, to live encamped in a thousand precautions, to be ever mindful of the newest frightening study and the latest life-extending health tip, ever alert to a thousand unlikely risks — as if all this makes any difference whatsoever to death. If death is the enemy, here's the most statistically correct answer to our fears: Drive carefully, eat a low-fat diet, don't smoke, and exercise regularly. But I think we are looking for something more profound to emerge from our experience.

At core, unwarranted fear is the fear of death. It frightened us that the 9/11 hijackers acted in spite of that natural fear, and there is great power in that ability. We, too, gain that power when we act in spite of our fear of death. All those who try to frighten us might benefit from recalling this truth: Everybody dies, but not everybody lives.

September 11 is our reminder to live — to live as fully as possible, and to live with less fear of one another than we used to.

September 11 is our reminder that we are nowhere near the limits of our compassion.

September 11 is our reminder to go to Disney World, to fly across the country on a surprise visit to loved ones, to go to New York and help "the city that never sleeps" sleep more soundly in the comfort of our support.

September 11 can be our annual reminder to do it now, whatever it is, say it now, whatever it is.

> Oh for a way to wake the dead;
> So much undone, so much unsaid.

This passage from a poem that was written by my father after the death of his father always makes me feel sadness about things I didn't express to some people in my life. At the same time, the poem gives me hope, for when I read "Oh for a way to wake the dead," I sometimes think, Oh for a way to wake the living!

That happened for many people on September 11, such that today it seems Americans are living more consciously than ever before, connected to one another more than at any time in our history. We have felt the sting of terrible violence, and the kindness it unleashed is ours for the keeping — if we stay awake. To do anything less than fully embrace the stunning opportunity we hold out to one another would be like waking up to a room full of smoke, opening the window to let it out, and then going back to sleep.

Those who hate us hope we do just that, for then pain and loss and fear would be the lasting results of our experience of terrorism. But thus far we've made another choice, a choice to see hazard only in those storm clouds where it exists, and to fly more freely in the clear skies between them. Our triumph over terror honors the thousands of people who died on September 11, and makes them heroes in a war we have already won.

ACKNOWLEDGMENTS

EVERY BOOK INVOLVES SOME STRESS, though few are written when everyone is under stress. The six weeks of writing that started in late September 2001 were made possible by many friends and associates who provided encouragement and support — during a time when we all had plenty of things on our minds, just as you did. Kathy Robbins, my friend and agent through four books (so far), always said the right words while I struggled to find so many right words. Bill Phillips edited my first book, and his teachings are part of everything I've written. I'm grateful to you, Bill, for clearing your schedule to join me again.

Speaking of clearing schedules, that's what people all over Little, Brown must have done to get a book printed and distributed on a schedule that contained just one date: Immediate. Thank you to Michael Pietsch and Geoff

Shandler. There were two people in America who could have done this, and you are the two.

To Sandi Mendleson: so smart, so effective, and such a great friend. I don't know how people get books out without you.

To Danelle Morton: Thank you for stopping so much to help me start so fast. Writing is lonely, and you made it less so.

To Garry Shandling: Thank you for a great lesson in friendship. Everything you did and said landed. To my dear friend and frustrating taskmaster, Andrew Jarecki: Thank you for what amounted to a mission statement. Eric Idle, you have no idea how much energy you gave me the day you visited, and the many other days I am blessed to get some time with you. Harry Shearer and Judith Owen: Your wisdom is on these pages (though you've probably got enough left for a brief appendix — and yes, Harry, I can hear some joke about that). Scott Gordon: You'll get thanked twice in this book, but just once in the next, okay? Ed Begley, Jr: Thanks for the meals you cooked, and the many more you offered.

To Olivia: You are inspiring whether I am writing or not. George: I thought I was working the hardest, but it was you, my friend.

Lance Richard, Fabian Dominguez, and Ron Eastman: You guys really showed compassion, to me and my friends — and that always hits the spot.

Michelle Pfeiffer and Oprah Winfrey: I'm sure you'll quickly recognize which chapters are in this book because of your encouragement.

To Michael LaFever: I have thanked you so many times in these twenty years that it may not mean much to you anymore. It means a lot to me, my friend. To the other friends I work with, thank you each for the extra support (and so many extra hours since 9/11): Robert Martin, Chuck Cogswell, Jeff Marquart, Ellen Prystajko, Dennis Kirvin, Caroline Murrey, Matt Slatoff, Ryan Martin, Gabrielle Thompson, David Falconer, Josh Dessalines, Raquel Matsubayashi, Paul Wright, Geoff Towle, Heather Ragsdale, Rob Nightengale, and all the others whose jobs (and names) are nonpublic. KMC: You know who you are, and who you are makes a big difference in my life.

For special insight and support: FDNY Captain Gerard Somerville, NYPD Sergeant John Egan, NYPD Lieutenant Jay Fagan, Stephanie and Peter S., Cliff Schuyler, Roman Pryjomko, Bankrobber, Mark Bryan, Heather Rizzo, Raymond Zilinskas, Red Thomas, Don Weisberg, MacKenzie B., Tony Robbins, Ron Iden, Rex Rakow, Eric Fernald, Steve Lamont, EJ Devokaitis, Geena Davis, Robert Miller, Jeff Jacobs, David Boulet, Bruce Wagner, Dad, Melissa, and Carrie Fisher (because what are acknowledgments without your name?).

Shaun Cassidy: You gave me a lot more than the title, particularly if I count the thirty years of best friendship.

And dear Alanis, I invite you to write books or songs about how to best support writers, because you've got that down. Write about how to best support a friend, because you've got that down, too. I live, I learn — better with you, and I love you so much.

THE ADVISORY BOARD
FOR *FEAR LESS*

I N WRITING THIS BOOK, I drew on experience, previous writings, new research, the work of my associates, and exceptional advisors. Our nation is now facing great challenges, so I sought out guidance from great experts. The members of the advisory board for this book gave their time and insight to help others. That's the same motivation I've seen them apply to the important work they do every day. I am grateful to each of them, as I know readers will be.

Gavin de Becker

Thomas A. Taylor

Lieutenant Taylor was recently named the Anti-Terrorism Coordinator for all operations of the Missouri State Highway Patrol. He was President of the National Governor's Security Association (NGSA) for four terms. During his twenty-nine years with the Patrol, he served in many senior positions, including Commander of the Governor's Security Division. Lieutenant Taylor is the Patrol's top expert in the MOSAIC threat-assessment system. He was among several leading threat-assessment experts chosen to serve on an advisory board to develop the new MOSAIC for Assessment of Public Figure Pursuit (MAPP).

Charles Cogswell

Chuck Cogswell served twenty-four years as a commissioned officer in the Military Police Corps of the U.S. Army, retiring at the rank of colonel. As the Chief of Security, Force Protection and Law Enforcement Division, he was responsible for the army's policies and programs for threat assessment, counterterrorism, physical security, and criminal investigation. He also commanded two of the largest districts in the U.S. Army Criminal Investigation Command (CID).

While deployed on Operation Desert Storm, Chuck performed critical threat assessments on U.S. forces' vulnerability to terrorist attack.

Chuck is Director of Threat Assessment and Management for Gavin de Becker and Associates.

Andrew L. Vita

Andy Vita is the former Assistant Director of the Bureau of Alcohol, Tobacco and Firearms, where he spent thirty-one years. Teams he created, equipped, and directed were successfully utilized at the sites of the World Trade Center bombing, the Oklahoma City federal building bombing, and the crash of TWA Flight 800.

Andy is now Executive Vice President at Armor Holdings, Inc.

Dr. James McGee

Dr. James McGee is a Special Consultant to the FBI's Critical Incident Response Group and Chief Psychologist of the Baltimore County Police Department. He directs psychological services programs for both the Maryland and Delaware State Police. He served for nineteen years as Director of Psychology and Forensic Services at Sheppard Pratt Hospital in Baltimore, Maryland.

Robert Martin

During his twenty-eight-year career with the Los Angeles Police Department, Robert Martin directed several of the department's most important responsibilities. He served as Commanding Officer of specialized detective divisions, including Commanding Officer of Detective Headquarters Division. In 1990, he founded the LAPD's Threat Management Unit, the first of its kind in the nation. He is a founding member of the Association of Threat Assessment Professionals.

Currently vice president of Gavin de Becker and Associates, Bob was a lead developer on the MOSAIC system co-designed by Gavin de Becker and the U.S. Marshals Service, now used for evaluating threats to federal judges.

He led the development team on the MOSAIC used for assessing domestic-violence situations and the MOSAIC system used for screening threats to public officials.

Dave Grossman

Lt. Col. Dave Grossman, U.S. Army (ret.) served as an Army Ranger, a West Point psychology professor, and a professor of military science. He is the author of *On Killing: The Psychological Cost of Learning to Kill in War and Society,* which is required reading in classes at West Point, the U.S. Air Force Academy, and police academies worldwide. Dave served as an expert witness and consultant in the case of *United States* v. *Timothy McVeigh*. His research was cited by President Clinton in a national address after the Littleton, Colorado, school shootings.

Frederick S. Calhoun

Frederick S. Calhoun was the lead researcher and principal developer of the threat-assessment process currently used by the U.S. Marshals Service for analyzing risks to federal judicial officials. Mr. Calhoun coordinated the curriculum and led a nationwide training program on contemporary threat management for local law-enforcement agencies. Mr. Calhoun earned his Ph.D. from the University of Chicago and is the author of eight books, including *Defusing the Risk to Judicial Officials: The Contemporary Threat Management Process* and *Hunters and Howlers: Threats and Violence Against Judicial Officials in the United States.*

Scott Gordon

Scott Gordon has worked in the criminal-justice system for nearly twenty-five years, as a police officer and detective for eight, and a prosecutor for the past sixteen. In 1997, he was selected as a legal advisor with the United Nations International War Crimes Tribunal, serving in Rwanda and at The Hague. He has been honored as Prosecuting Attorney of the Year, and is a nationally recognized expert in issues involving intimate violence. He served six terms as Chairman of the Domestic Violence Council.

He is a professor of law at Southwestern University.

Michael D. Carrington

Mike has been U.S. Marshal for Northern Indiana since his appointment by President Clinton in 1994.

He was Director of Campus Security at Indiana University South Bend for fifteen years, and adjunct associate professor in the School of Public and Environmental Affairs, teaching criminal-justice courses.

He is a member of the Association of Threat Assessment Professionals.

Peter G. Herley

During his thirty-four-year career in law enforcement, Peter Herley served with the Torrance Police Department, commanding various divisions. He has been President of the California Police Chiefs Association (CPCA), and most recently, chief of police in the town of Tiburon, California. He is widely recognized for his involvement in programs that improve relations between the police and communities.

Chief Herley serves on the advisory board of the International Institute of Criminal Justice Leadership at the University of San Francisco and coordinates courses for new chiefs of police, taught by the California Commission on Peace Officers Standards and Training (POST).

He is president of Herley Consulting, located in San Rafael, California.

Cappy Gagnon

Among his many law-enforcement and security positions, Cappy Gagnon was Executive Assistant to the Los Angeles County Sheriff, Director of Special Programs for the department, and Assistant Director of the Police Executive Institute of the Police Foundation, of Washington, D.C. He is currently a coordinator of security and Manager of Special Event Security for the University of Notre Dame.

Paul Mones

Paul Mones is an attorney and author. He has a nationwide practice devoted to representing children, and he is the author of *When a Child Kills.* Mr. Mones conducts lectures and training throughout the country on issues relating to child abuse, delinquency, and family violence.

· Appendix A ·

WEB SITES FOR UP-TO-DATE INFORMATION

NEWS SOURCES

www.eclecticesoterica.com/news.html
News Web site with links to the top twenty-five newspapers in the world, local newspapers and television stations in every region internationally, many of them in English. Also links to major U.S. news sources such as the *New York Times, Washington Post,* CNN, etc. Useful for developing your own international perspective on the news.

www.assignmenteditor.com/index.cfm
Links to national and international news publications, media outlets, government organizations, and Web sites for news in business, entertainment, politics, and media as well as sites that feature the local concerns of specific large cities. Specific link to a page designed to gather resources related to the 9/11 disaster.

www.miis.edu

Perspectives on the conflict from academics who have international political, diplomatic and espionage backgrounds, from the faculty of the Monterey Institute of International Studies.

www.janes.com/

Articles about the conflict in Afghanistan from a weapons-manufacturing perspective: strategies, alliances. Coverage of military actions and tactics by countries besides the United States. Weapons analyzed include biochem.

www.alertnet.org

Breaking news from Reuters about war, aid, disasters.

SECURITY

www.firstgov.gov

Central home page for all national government links. Search by topic to find latest government thinking on the state of the crisis. For example, www.firstgov.gov/featured/usgresponse offers protection tips for mail, anthrax, bombs; a place to report leads and clues; and an emergency contact list.

www.whitehouse.gov/homeland

Office of Homeland Security. Press releases about government activities, speeches. Straightforward information on emergency preparedness.

www.usps.gov
Updates on mail, safe handling of mail, and government positions on mail handling.

www.ccmostwanted.com/mostwantedterr.htm
America's most wanted cyberterrorists, with pictures. E-mail or phone (1-866-483-5137).

www2.sbccom.army.mil
Military's description of its preparations.

www.epa.gov
Water-supply security, air-quality-monitoring tables, FAQ, anthrax.

www.fbi.gov
Information on the hunt for the terrorists, most-wanted photos, rewards for information leading to the capture of bin Laden, anthrax cases. Link to place to leave tips. To report information over the Internet: www.ifccfbi.gov or phone 1-800-CRIMETV

www.ndpo.gov
The clearinghouse for state, local, and federal weapons of mass destruction information. Training materials and fact sheets.

www.stimson.org
Private research institute that focuses on issues of national and international security. Site offers analysis of bioterrorism: proliferation throughout the world, history, FAQs.

www.hhs.gov
Department of Health and Human Services home page: anthrax, Cipro availability, how to get help if affected by biological terrorism.

www.anser.org
Private research institute that publishes its own journal on homeland security with articles written by major government figures and academics. Journal is called *Homeland Security Journal,* but is not to be confused with the government Office of Homeland Security. Site also offers links to academic and private institutions that study this issue.

PSYCHOLOGICAL STRESS

www.aacap.org/publications/disasterresponse/index.htm
American Academy of Child and Adolescent Psychiatry on how to talk to children about 9/11, other disasters, news watching.

www.ces.purdue.edu
Purdue University Extension program articles on how to discuss terrorism with children.

www.nimh/nih.gov/publicat/violence.cfm
National Institute of Mental Health recommendations on helping children and adolescents cope with violence and disaster.

www.helping.apa.org/daily/terrorism.html
General recommendations on how terrorism affects us psychologically, warning signs of stress, and how to cope with trauma.

AIRLINE SAFETY

www.airlinesafety.com
Opinionated forum for discussing policies and issues related to airline safety. With articles, editorials, letters, and links.

www.airsafe.com
Provides safety data and advice for traveling on passenger airplanes, including accident-news articles, tips, and weather reports. Specific articles about the status of reinforced cockpit doors on different airlines, airport-security issues, in-flight transportation of chemicals, suspicious mail. Separate section about rumors and misinformation.

www.airsafetyonline.com
Up-to-date news on security breaches, airport status, and recent crashes.

http://www.faa.gov
Security regulations, requirements for flying, what you can carry on board.

www.ntsb.gov
Descriptions of major accidents and recent accident reports. Investigations, statistics, formal results of accident reports.

EMERGENCY PREPAREDNESS

www.cdc.gov/nceh/emergency/prev_em.htm
Centers for Disease Control recommendations on disaster preparedness.

www.fema.gov/pte/prep.htm
How to prepare for a variety of disasters.

www.noaa.gov
National Oceanic and Atmospheric Administration information on natural disasters, storm watch, ozone layer, with satellite imagery.

www.usgs.gov
Hurricanes, extreme storms, volcanoes, earthquakes, with links to preparedness recommendations.

www.esri.com
Hazard awareness. Allows you to make a hazard map of your area or one you may be visiting.

RELIEF EFFORTS AND DONATIONS

www.uwnyc.org/sep11/
United Way of New York City donation site:
The September 11th Fund
United Way of New York City
2 Park Avenue
New York, NY 10016
U.S.A.
1-800-710-8002

www.nypfwc.org/
New York City Police and Fire
Widows' and Children's Fund
P.O. Box 3713
Grand Central Station
New York, NY 10163

www.fema.gov
Latest on relief efforts, how to apply for relief or donate funds.

www.redcross.org
Latest on relief efforts around the world, disaster-preparedness tips, first aid information, how to donate money, blood, tissue. Links to other helpful sites.

www.reliefweb.int/w/rwb.nsf
International perspective on humanitarian relief efforts.

BIO-TERRORISM

www.anthrax.osd.mil/
Department of Defense anthrax site.

www.cdc.gov/
Centers for Disease Control main page: latest press releases, state of the nation, information on anthrax and other biological agents.

wwwbt.cdc.gov
CDC page specific to bio-terrorism. Regularly updated.

www.hopkins-biodefense.org/
Johns Hopkins University Schools of Medicine and Public
Health *Information for Clinicians on Anthrax; JAMA* consensus statements on botulinum toxin, plague, smallpox, tularemia; concise diagnostic criteria and treatment guidelines
for anthrax, botulism, smallpox and plague; how to handle
anthrax threat letters; BT preparedness and response post-Sept. 11; FAQ: information for the general public.

www.fda.gov/
Government information on approved drugs for various
bioagents.

www.who.int/home-page/
Health status of refugees and Afghanistan, world recommendations on vaccinations such as smallpox, advisories
about "deliberate infections" — meaning bio-terrorism.

www.osha.gov/
Mail-handling recommendations, air-quality-monitoring
information for those working at the World Trade Center
from the Occupational Safety and Health Administration.

www.bact.wisc.edu/Bact330/lectureanthrax
Anthrax history, photos, information.

www.ama-assn.org/special/infohome.htm
Journal of the American Medical Association search: excellent
site for research on bio-terrorism, history, vaccines.

· Appendix B ·

TALKING TO CHILDREN ABOUT TERRORISM

M Y FRIEND AND COLLEAGUE Paul Mones is a wise attorney and author who has dedicated his life to protecting the rights of children. Paul wrote the seminal book on children who kill (*When a Child Kills*). In his research and his law practice, he has met many children who were profoundly traumatized. Accordingly, he has an extraordinary inside look at how children react to great stress and fear. I asked Paul to share some of his thoughts on how to best approach children's fears about terrorism.

GdeB

· · ·

Perhaps the single most important factor that determines how we as human beings deal with fear is age. Children, especially those under thirteen, are highly vulnerable members of our society in this regard because they lack the intellectual and emotional capacity to process fear in the ways that adults can. Because children have no significant life history upon which to reflect and compare current events, they are more easily prone to misinterpret the meaning of those events and have an exaggerated response to them. Vast numbers of adults watching repeated newscasts of the Twin Towers collapsing during the first few days following September 11 were seeing something that was clearly traumatic, but a number of very young children who saw the same repeated images actually believed that the attacks were happening over and over again.

As adults we are responsible for helping our children cope with the aftermath of 9/11. And the first step is to realize that you cannot help your child unless you first help yourself. You set your child's emotional compass. Your child relies upon you to navigate through these rough waters. When dads or moms are nervous and anxious, their kids know it — immediately. Remember the warning you get on an airplane about the oxygen masks: "If you are traveling with a young child, first put the mask on yourself, then assist your child." Similarly, you are your child's anchor — take care of yourself first.

As you manage your own fears and build new strengths in the times ahead, there are a number of concrete things you can do to help your children. These brief suggestions are aimed primarily at helping the most vulnerable children, those under thirteen, but they can be applied to helping teens as well.

■   ■   ■

While we cannot nor should we completely shield children from post-9/11 events, we must screen how much information they receive. To this end, as many experts have said, don't let young children watch TV news. Television news is, to say the least, not kid-friendly. If there had ever been any question in your mind before September 11, there should be no question now: TV news is not intended for youthful consumption. It is purposefully intended to intellectually and emotionally engage the viewer on a level young children simply have not as yet attained.

Perhaps just as damaging as watching the television news is for children to hear their parents and other adults discuss disturbing news events. Be careful what you say to other adults in person or on the phone when children are present. And do not assume that they don't hear you merely because they are in another room. Their ears have tiny radar for the tones of agitation or distress in a parent's voice. And if you are sharing your anxiety and bits of news with friends on the phone, they're getting it, even if they don't actually hear the words — even if they don't completely understand the words. It will be difficult to convince them to remain calm when they see and feel your agitation. So do the best you can to reserve your expressions of anxiety and fear for when they are sleeping or out of the house.

I am not advocating keeping your children completely in the dark. Inevitably children will hear things from other adults or friends or directly witness certain events in their lives, like armed troops on bridges or in airports. It is therefore your responsibility to become a current-events translator for your child. There are two things you know about any news report: First, you are likely not getting the whole story, and second, whatever you hear today may change tomorrow and may change again next week. Witness the information roller coaster surrounding the anthrax problem. One strategy is to reduce the events of the day to their simplest, most logical common denominator. For example: The soldiers we have fighting for the United States are like the policemen you see every day. Police protect us from people who may want to hurt us in America, soldiers protect us when people from other countries may want to hurt us. As for the anthrax scare: Somebody put some bad stuff in a few letters, and some people who opened them got sick. But you have to remember that there are billions and billions of letters sent every week, and only a very, very few of them had that bad stuff in them. You have nothing to worry about because everybody is doing everything they can to make the mail safe and catch the people who put the bad stuff in the mail.

In explaining terrorism to children, it is much more important for children to know about all the people who will protect them from anything bad happening than it is to know what some terrorist can do to hurt them. Let's be honest: Few of us can fully grasp the nature of the terrorist threat or all the issues of foreign extremists. So stick with what you know. Children should be told that their protection and safety is the most important thing not only to Mommy and Daddy but to the President of the United States and all the people who help him run the country.

In these times one of the best salves for all of us, and especially your children, is to go back to what you can rely upon: your family's history and that of the United States. Tell your children that your mom and dad protected you in tough times and that your grandparents protected your parents during similar times. In fact, if the children's grandparents (or for that matter, any elderly person) are available, ask them to tell your child the same thing. What parents do best is protect their children. It's what you have been doing since your child was born, and you're not going to stop now. Tell your children stories of resiliency. Tell them about their ancestors who survived wars, slavery, or the depression. Hope about the future lies in the strength of the past. You can tell them whatever stories out of history have inspired you, but just make the stories age-appropriate, which usually means short and simple, for that is what a child best understands.

It is difficult being a wise parent even in easy times, and it's especially difficult now. Your job will be made easier if you involve yourself and your children in any of the wonderful community projects that have come out of this terrible tragedy. One of the most comforting things for children is to know that they aren't alone, that they don't have to face the future by themselves. As important as it is to help your children deal with their fear, it is equally critical to involve them in all the good that has been produced from these horrific events. You can chose numerous ways to involve your children: becoming part of a school or community project writing letters to public servants who acted and continue to act so heroically in responding to 9/11 (firefighters, police officers, etc.), collecting money for refugee or survivor relief, etc. Whatever you chose to do together with your child will make your child stronger and will bring your child the good that can always be found in difficult times. Just seeing you prevail so well can be a valuable experience that stays with your child for a lifetime.

Paul Mones

(Some resources about talking to children and teens are offered in Appendix A.)

ESSAY ON HOW 9/11 AFFECTED PEOPLE OF DIFFERENT AGES

CHRIS MATTHEWS is a writer and syndicated colum-
nist you may know best from his popular television
show, *Hardball*.

Washington — For some reason, this anthrax scare is
tougher on younger people. It's the people in their twen-
ties who fret the loudest. They wait on line to be tested.
They want their Cipro. They want people like me to stop
our "denial."

They are puzzled by older people's reactions, as em-
bodied by the angry defiance of Tom Brokaw and Tom
Daschle.

It's a generational thing, and I have my suspicions about
why.

One theory is that we older people have been through
worse. Some still hide jars of quarters in the basement for

fear of another Great Depression. World War II and Korea took men from the classroom and threw them into battle. The early Cold War had kids huddled under our desks waiting for the big "flash" that meant the beginning of World War III — and the end of the world.

Then came Vietnam. That war cost ten times the number of American lives than the World Trade Center attacks. Some young men went to Vietnam willingly and courageously. Some were grabbed and found the courage for the fight. Some just sweated it out back home. You think anthrax was bad? You should have seen the draft.

My second suspicion is more subtle. It has to do with loss. When I came to Washington thirty years ago last spring, you could walk right into the office of any senator or member of Congress. You could go anywhere you wanted in the Capitol any time of day. There were no metal detectors, no ID cards to show, nothing. The right to petition Congress was as literal as it says in the Constitution. You wanted to pester some politician, you went ahead and did it.

The same was true of the president. The no. 33 bus from Friendship Heights drove right in front of the White House on the way to Capitol Hill. When President Richard Nixon got into trouble, a driver could honk his horn as he passed 1600 Pennsylvania Ave. and the occupant upstairs knew it meant, "Resign!"

All this is gone.

Now, checkpoints dot the Capitol plaza where FDR said we have nothing to fear but fear itself. You can't drive a truck anywhere near the Hill. Pennsylvania Avenue is closed to traffic from 15th Street to 17th Street.

Even the air has a perimeter. If anyone leaves their seat during the thirty-minute approach to Reagan National Airport, the plane may head directly to Dulles.

Want to write your senator? Forget it. That anthrax-tainted letter to Tom Daschle from Trenton virtually shut down the Capitol.

It took years for this shutting of the democratic gates. First came the bombing in the Capitol in '71. Then Oklahoma City. Then September 11 and United Flight 93, the fourth plane that may have been headed for the Capitol, but was brought down by courageous passengers.

This thing called terrorism has wormed its way into our collective consciousness. Anthrax spores are in the Senate mail. Little particles of hell are in the Capitol air. Staffers with nervous systems once wired to the news cycle now wait in line for Cipro. The big questions of foreign policy and fiscal policy have shrunk to the small one: How do I stay alive?

"We have some planes," we hear a hijacker say. "Just stay quiet and you'll be OK — nobody move, please — don't try to make any stupid moves."

We older people refuse to buy it. Maybe it's because we've been through worse. Maybe because we've been through better.

Chris Matthews

· Appendix D ·

GAVIN DE BECKER AND ASSOCIATES

G AVIN DE BECKER and Associates is a seventy-member firm that advises clients on the assessment and management of threats of violence, inappropriate pursuit, stalking situations, workplace violence, biological attack, and terrorism.

The Threat Assessment and Management Division (TAM) assesses inappropriate, alarming, or threatening communications and develops management plans for dealing with unwanted pursuers and safety hazards. TAM also conducts sensitive investigations relevant to safety and assists clients with strategies to reduce their vulnerability to inappropriate pursuit and to enhance privacy. TAM provides expert-witness consultation on cases involving stalking, threats, and prevention of violence. This division runs the special team that surveys sites and screens mail for the presence of biological pathogens.

The MOSAIC® Threat Assessment Systems Division provides advanced training to law enforcement, prosecutors, state and federal agencies, corporate executives, and school administrators on threat assessment, case management, and the prevention of violence. MOSAIC refers to a computer-assisted threat-assessment method that helps ensure fairness, consistency, and thoroughness. MOSAIC systems designed for specific assessment applications are available to government agencies, universities, school systems, corporations, and some other institutions:

- MAPP-MOSAIC for Assessment of Public Figure Pursuit
- MDV-MOSAIC for Assessment of Domestic Violence Situations
- MAST-MOSAIC for Assessment of School Threats
- MAST-U-MOSAIC for Assessment of School Threats in a University Setting
- MAT-W-MOSAIC for Assessment of Threats in the Workplace
- JUDICIAL-MOSAIC for Assessment of Judicial Threats

The Protective Security Division (PSD) provides advance planning and coordination, logistical support, and protective coverage for public figures and other at-risk individuals. Protective coverage is provided at public appearances, while traveling, as well as round-the-clock protection at private residences and corporate offices. PSD also provides secure transportation using highly trained drivers and specially equipped armored vehicles.

The Technical Security Services Division (TSS) conducts security surveys of residences and offices, providing detailed written recommendations for improvement. TSS reviews plans, coordinates with security vendors, and develops installation specifications for security enhancements.

Three times a year, Gavin de Becker and Associates gathers leading experts to conduct advanced training in threat assessment and management for government officials, law-enforcement professionals, university police, and corporate security personnel. These four-day academies are held at the UCLA Conference Center at Lake Arrowhead, California.

For additional information regarding Gavin de Becker and Associates, visit: www.gavindebecker.com.

Or contact:

Infoline@gavindebecker.com

Gavin de Becker and Associates
11684 Ventura Blvd., #440
Studio City, CA 91604

Fax: (818) 506-0426

Mr. de Becker's share of profits from royalties from the sale of this book go to improving threat-assessment capabilities and to Victory Over Violence, a charity that provides direct support to families affected by violence.

Victory Over Violence
15332 Antioch Street, No. 507
Pacific Palisades, CA 90272
www.victoryoverviolence.com